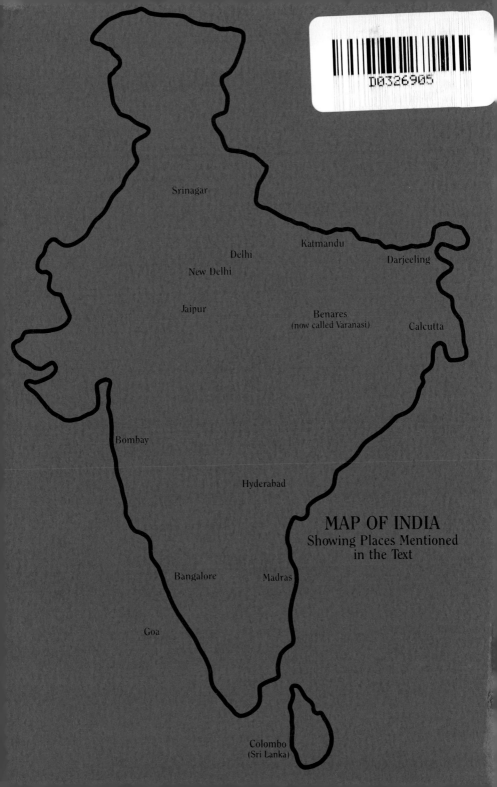

D0326905

Srinagar

Katmandu

Delhi

Darjeeling

New Delhi

Jaipur

Benares
(now called Varanasi)

Calcutta

Bombay

Hyderabad

MAP OF INDIA
Showing Places Mentioned
in the Text

Bangalore

Madras

Goa

Colombo
(Sri Lanka)

TRAVELS
THROUGH
THE
MIND
OF
INDIA

Also by Barbara Brown

*Stress and the
Art of Biofeedback*

New Mind/New Body

*Supermind:
The Ultimate Energy*

TRAVELS THROUGH THE

MIND *of* INDIA

by Barbara Brown

Saybrook

Publishing Company

Dallas   San Francisco   New York

Library of Congress Cataloging-in-Publication Data

Brown, Barbara B.
  Travels through the mind of India.
  1. India—Religion—20th century.
  2. Brown, Barbara B.—Journeys—India.
  3. India—Description and travel—1947-1980.
  4. India—Description and travel—1981-
  I. Title.
  II. Title: Mind of India.
  BL2007.7.B76   1987   294'.0954   86-43045
  ISBN 0-933071-11-6

Saybrook Publishing Co., Inc.
4223 Cole Avenue, Suite Four, Dallas, TX 75205

Printed in the United States of America

Distributed by W.W. Norton & Company
500 Fifth Avenue, New York, NY 10110

CONTENTS

MEETING
THE MIND OF INDIA

In India people heed psychic rhythms just as in the West we follow our biological rhythms. In the Western approach to life, with its security locked into the physical structure of the universe, scientific experts define "biological clocks", the rhythmic shifting of biological activities at intervals of hours or days or even years. But in India it is spiritual activity that counts, and *their* experts concentrate on characterizing *spiritual* rhythms. And because the soul is eternal, its cycles can only try to split infinity.

It is not easy to cross the cultural barrier between East and West, to move from where one's life is tuned to office clocks and changing seasons to a consciousness focused on psychic hopes and dreams. To move from a social milieu that is, for the most part, subject to the conditions of its physical nature into a society preoccupied by its spiritual destiny means

that the way one perceives one's world must change profoundly.

There are signs that we of the West are broadening our
powers of perception and developing new ways to perceive
the world around us. We are becoming more sensitive and
more aware and we now talk about "being open", a useful
new mind tool for expanding interpersonal relationships.
When you analyze what "being open" means, you discover it
means not only the willingness to talk and to listen, but it
means also *to listen differently.*

We in the West have all been taught, for example, to
see time linearly, in sequences, with no dimensions to manipu-
late, and to think of space as static, neither expandable nor
compressible. We have been taught to seek a cause for every
effect, tracing the flow of events linearly to be sure to identify
"causal relationships". Historically, in contrast, in India time
and space, cause and effect, are perceived very differently, in
relationships defined by experience and manipulations by the
meditative mind.

What we call the "immutable" laws of our natural
universe are violated in the psychic networking and spiritual
time of India. The laws may be violated, but none of us, Indian
or Westerner (except the true believers), knows for sure
which world is the reality. In Indian philosophy, of course, the
physical universe is "maya" (illusion), while in the West new
findings in quantuum mechanics challenge our older, fixed
notions of what the physical world really is.

I have become convinced that no amount of study can
lead to a truly meaningful appreciation of the Indian mind.
After long exposure to Indian culture, I have come to agree

with the Indian philosophers that the "experiential", the *experience* of the slow thrust of Indian times and space, of Indian history and beliefs, provides the sole avenue for meaningful appreciation of the way the Indian perceives life. It was, perhaps, my own karma that led me so frequently around the byroads of India and commanded my psyche to find a way to ease the crossing of the cultural barrier from West to East.

Then, just as slowly as I had grown to perceive the Indian life and mind behind their worldly masks, I began to realize that other people would need, perhaps, as broad an Indian experience as I had had before they could feel comfortable and at home with the Indian mind. I decided to extract samples of my adventures with this very different way of life and present them much as I had lived them. Although each piece describes a tiny slice of a Westerner's mind travels through India, each can only whisper its meanings. Taken together, however, I hope the sum will help the reader to absorb the subtle, complex flavors of the Indian mind and psyche.

The Beginning

My life and times in India have been enveloped in a supernatural cloak. No, there have not been any wondrous, notable episodes of clairvoyance or teleportation or psychometry. Rather, each lengthy visit has been lightly blessed by continuing, enchanting experiences, each of which is strange and difficult to explain but none (save one or two) could be said to be evidence for supernatural influences.

On the other hand, the repeated occurrence of such shadowy psychic-like experiences set me to wonder until I finally began to understand that something very real, although unsubstantial, was happening whenever I set foot in India. When I describe this curious phenomenon to other serious visitors to India, nearly everyone exclaims in agreement. Unquestionably, our relationships with minds and time and space are very different in India. What I began to recognize was that there was a *pattern* of events occurring that literally forced my mind to pay attention to the nature of these subtle events and to try to understand what was going on.

It all began with my very first visit to India in 1970. I had been invited by the Czechoslovakian government to participate in an international brain conference dealing with the neurophysiology of images. Since my expenses were being paid and included an around-the-world airfare, I decided to detour by way of India and visit Calcutta to see dear friends, the Drs. Ranjan and Kanak Dasgupta, husband and wife physicians whom I had met while they were on exchange fellowships to UCLA. I managed a few touristy weeks in Bombay and Delhi before flying up to Nepal, then finally on to Calcutta.

My strange adventures in India began in India's air space, long before the plane actually touched down. I had caught cold in Katmandu and my condition was deteriorating rapidly, so in the emergency I booked on the first available flight to Calcutta and my physician friends. There was not, however, time to notify them about my sudden change in plans. To add to the difficulty, the normally short flight took more than seven hours. No sooner on board than there was a strange buzzing among the passengers, followed shortly by an announcement that we would clear customs at Patna. It was a time of great tension between India and Nepal, and the Indian airport bureaucrats took the customs regulation as an opportunity to harass the Nepalese. It took some four hours for the twenty-five passengers to clear customs into India.

It was a miserable afternoon but only a portent of what was to come. We arrived at Calcutta's Dum-Dum airport around 8 P.M. Our plane parked half a mile from the airport buildings and we were led, by the dimmest of lights, along dirt paths to a very old and little-used open building where I gathered our luggage would be delivered. There was virtually no one about. I looked around for a taxi and discovered not a car of any kind in sight. I was too sick to panic. Finally, in the shadows, I spotted an antiquated bus. It had no lights at all, inside or out.

Just then I heard a shout and saw the luggage being thrown on a low concrete parapet that served as a baggage claim area. Clouds of white-clad Indians stormed the parapet grabbing at bags. I could find no one to help me, but my fright urged me on and I managed to recover all five of my pieces of luggage (oh foolish tourist!). The Indians were all heading for the bus and, with another surge of adrenalin, I managed to grasp all my possessions and board the bus. I had no idea where it was going. Logically, I told myself, it was the only way out.

It was an eerie kind of darkness. The bus still had no lights and the passengers made almost no sound at all. Finally the bus coughed and started.

The trip into Calcutta became the experience of a lifetime, a memorable, soul-stirring encounter with an ancestral
drama of the Indian heart and soul. The countryside was a
mass of white-clothed Indians. Thousands upon thousands
were camped alongside every road and in every parkway. The
tableau stretched on and on, for at least ten miles. I would
never again see such a massive pilgrimage. Each group had
their heavy string cots and cooking pots and some had brought
livestock. Food was cooking everywhere over fires made from
cow dung patties. The air was thick with their acrid smoke that
hung in dense clouds over us, like fishnets thrown against the
sky. It became hard to breathe. Still, I have never seen such
a sight and I was literally frozen with incredulity. What, indeed, was the spirit and dedication that moved these pilgrims
to endure such difficulties? It was an awesome scene to experience.

My entry adventure was not yet over. At what appeared to be the very center of Calcutta, the bus stopped and
in a horrendous jumble of push-shove-throw, the passengers
all landed curbside amongst a pile of luggage. Trying to grab
my luggage I found myself struggling against a mass of brown
sweaty bodies tearing at me and my luggage. Just as I was
about to collapse with a primal scream, an elderly Indian
gentleman appeared, uttered a single word, and the mass of
humanity fell from me and disappeared into the shadows.

"Let me get you a taxi," he said.

How marvelous it is to be rescued from the ravages of
beasts. The taxi took me to my hotel (naturally I had chosen
an Indian hotel). It was obviously not deluxe and appeared to
be the headquarters of a Red Chinese contingent (that's what

we called the Chinese in those days). Once in my room, I tumbled, dog-sick, into bed, too sick to care there were no towels or pillows. I was nearly asleep when the telephone rang. My friends, the two Dasguptas, had called every hotel in Calcutta and finally found me. They knew I was due in sometime during the week and would find a hotel, but they had suddenly been seized by fear for my safety and felt it was urgent to find me. Once more some psychic synchrony had saved me. Almost.

Ranjan and Kanak sped to my rescue. Each was armed with a black doctor's bag, ready to minister to my ills. But alas, India's economy then prohibited import of foreign drugs and there were no antibiotics, not even old-fashioned sulfa drugs. We tried to make do with native remedies, but they were far too feeble. Ever since then my faith in Indian medicine has been spotty despite my intellectual desire to believe in ancient remedies. It was a most difficult week in Calcutta and finally we all agreed I would not get well until I was home with proper medical care.

When I left India to come home after that first visit, I did so sadly, with bad feelings. The India I had found was filthy, insane, incompetent, uncaring, smelly and stupid. Much of my first visit had been totally miserable, particularly in Calcutta, beginning with the unceremonious, appalling treatment upon arrival at Dum-Dum airport until leaving time when the airline agent threw my luggage on a steel pinion, ripped it and insisted that his mending it with Scotch tape would see the luggage safely to Tokyo (it didn't of course). Once home I vowed never, *NEVER* to return to India.

Yet here is what I wrote three months later.

"As I prepared to leave India, I was aware of a strange uneasiness of mind. My feelings about the events that occurred there have not yet fallen into place. My unrest cannot be, I feel sure, a sadness one feels upon leaving precious places and people nor the making of memories to serve a later nostalgia. My feelings are, in fact, strangely absent of sorrow or regret.

"I feel no loss for lush landscapes or clean architecture that reflects man's elegance, or for the human warmth cast by contented faces. India has few such values that speak of individual man and his victories over nature. To the Westerner India is an ancient and raw land, peopled by brown, barefoot gnomes and genies wise in the magic of fantasy wherein the elements of earth and universe exist only for transmutations by the mind."

With a determination to understand my unrest upon leaving India, I began to search my inner thoughts. I found opinions and social prejudice, layers of emotional debris accumulated from years of uncritically absorbing provincial gossip until finally, cleansed from social dusts and away from the pressures of my Western world, I found my inner mind. Now unobstructed, the pathways from the eyes and ears and nose let Indian scenes pour in. Indian masses moved in and out of my memory images, foreign in their movements, smells and colors, yet locking themselves into bits of intelligence and mind stuff and fantasy.

My senses, stripped, were led again through the bareness and people-mass and poverty to the psychic substance that is India. In this contemplative reverie I began to soak up ways of life and the complexities of the curious people-geography,

absorbing auras of eternal pilgrimages to an unseen consciousness, a pilgrimage that marks India as clearly as MacDonalds
mark the United States. My mind and perceptions, my entire
being became flooded with liberated sensory notes; inner consciousness became occupied absorbing information, turning it
over and around, studying it until consciousness became
wholly enveloped by the Indian psyche.

I began then to plot how I could return to India.

The Time and Spaces and Mind of India

I have long had a deep curiosity about why India is the
way it is, about what gave rise to not just one, but two, of the
world's most widely followed religious philosophies so many
thousands of years ago, systems of thought and ethics that have
endured so long. And could the very different philosophies
about the meaning of life alone account for the striking difference in the way the two cultures of East and West have developed? Was the way of life in India truly, fundamentally different from the way of life in the West?

Now that so much of the West's psychology and medicine has adopted Indian mind techniques to discipline the
body for healing and wellness and fitness, would the West
come also to adopt the philosophy that underlies yoga, the
belief in supremacy of mind and spirit with the material world
held as more illusory than real? Western attitudes about the
meaning of life have certainly changed remarkably in the last
decade since yoga and meditation have become officially
recommended as mind and body health practices. For many,
the psychic values of life, the psychological and spiritual

values, have replaced material values. I began to wonder whether life experiences in the West might eventually come to be as transcendent of time and space as those in India.

As a scientist I had been taught that all human nature was basically the same, and that people of different cultures differed mainly in their belief systems and in the way beliefs affected the nonphysical values of life. Physical events, I was taught, are much the same the world over. I felt quite sure that all the *physical* factors that determine life were the same in India as at home. Certainly time and space and the physical world must be the same. Yet after only one visit to India, I began to question my Western notions.

Curiosity first sent me to India, but it was some strange magnetic force that kept me returning, and very much against my will. It took nearly ten lengthy tours of India before I became convinced that the phenomena surrounding me on each occasion were brushes with a different reality.

A good part of my inner argument concerned the tradition of science that demands documenting all observations about a phenomenon in ways that can be verified by others, and then drawing conclusions about the phenomenon that fit absolutely with what else we are sure of about the universe. I ended my struggle over the need to understand my Indian adventures scientifically when I finally admitted that events in India are structured very differently than in the West. By this time (also a curious coincidence), I had become a modest expert in the new pattern analysis techniques, those complex techniques that identify phenomena by the interaction of many different influences instead of the conventional scientific method that examines only one influence at a time. This new perspective on the nature of natural phenomena helped me to understand that time and space may, indeed, flow differently in India.

The following mind adventures, thus, describe my encounters with the minds and time and spaces of India. Each is a part of the whole phenomenon and while no single experience provides convincing proof for a different time-space reality in Indian life, each experience does tend to strengthen the notion that life events in India are very much different from those in our own reality. Looking at these mind adventures as a whole, linked by their setting, and seeing them as a whole pattern of experience, can generate quite new insights into the chameleon nature of human consciousness, both Indian and our own.

India has always stood in sharp contrast to all other countries on earth. It is the only great land area connected to the rest of earth that is nonetheless isolated. To the north, the massive Himalayas guard against contact with both friends and invaders, while two great oceans join to envelop the rest of the subcontinent between the Arabian Sea on the west and the prodigious Bay of Bengal to the east. The effect of India's eternal geographic isolation has been the development of a special brand of human nature and a unique human behavior.

The beliefs in India we call the philosophy of life or religious are not at all the same kind of believing as in the West. India *accepts* a universal spiritual potential for all life; the West holds there is potential for good *and* evil in everyone. In the Indian philosophy there is no good or evil, only fulfilling and not fulfilling. It is difficult for most Westerners to accept the Indian's traditional lack of active concern about good and evil. From its earliest times, Hindu philosophy has concentrated on the personal ethics of control of mind and body, non-attachment, reverence, forbearance, and concentration, believing that *social* ethics are possible only in an environment of righteous individuals. Concern for the individual psyche has always been a prime influence in Indian society and despite the perception of everyone being alone in a crowd in India, it is, nonetheless, exactly that provision for individual time their spiritual behavior fosters along with the consensus of a billion people-years that impress the reality of oneness and identity with the universal consciousness upon the visitor's psyche. For 5000 years the Hindu has been surrounded by the universal understanding that all life can bear divine fruit and that all life is a part of all other life.

The West, on the other hand, puts different bits of life into many different categories—the invertebrates, the amphibia, the primates (prime, of course), as well as Asian, Negroid, Aryan, Jew or Aborigine. Each is separate, non-aligned in the cosmic consciousness, and with strict criteria about who is eligible for heaven and when.

The differences between effects of Eastern and Western culture on human life are much more profound than most people realize. In the West one inherits the feeling of being an alien trying to enter a heavenly kingdom on earth, while in India, the weight of culture imbues one with the *sensation* of being part of the universal consciousness. More than intellectual conclusions, more than emotional attachments, these "sensations of knowing" seem to be understanding and awareness by the whole inner being. Not only are the psyches and the very being of East and West peoples organized so very differently, their wholly opposite views of consciousness and divinity and purpose of life make mutual understanding enormously difficult.

We have little opportunity to live and experience each other to achieve mutual understanding. India is so far away, with such a different standard of living and different way of life, we Westerners have come to rely on those few with leisure or interest enough to explore India and who also have the time and talent to report. Otherwise we must rely on the academicians' view of India with its investigatory and statistical descriptions that give little insight into the heart and soul of India and her people.

Insights gained from personal experience are also both rare and difficult. There is a profound effect on a single, isolated individual who must survive, however briefly, within a "cultural mass" such as hundreds of millions of Indians or Chinese or Russians. The visitor, the traveller and the immigrant to any foreign culture is a fragile spirit in a sea of very different ways of valuing life and one's place in life. Sociologists speak of this effect as "cultural shock," an unfortunately negative description of cultural interactions while psychologists talk about the need to adapt or adjust to new and different environments. Neither expresses the remarkable changes that occur within the human psyche when it must interact with a cultural mass.

That interaction occurs on at least two levels: consciously recognizing new environmental elements that generate reasons for the likes and dislikes of peoples and places. These generally superficial impressions often also shape the intellectual appraisal of a different culture.

It is the other level of cultural interaction that can lead to a true appreciation of the sense of a different culture. This is the quasi-unconscious adjustment to the new environment. Whether by accident or choice, when one is surrounded by a cultural mass such as that of India, the mind cannot begin to cope with the maze of implications every nuance of the culture arouses. The mind processes the information slowly, most of the impressions slipping past the conscious mind down into the storage bins of the subliminal mind. Gradually the hidden intellect fits the bits of information together and the psyche begins to flow with understanding. One is absorbing the weight of centuries of Indian philosophy and experiences the Hindu concept of consciousness, if only vicariously, and it is a concept and an experience that embraces a different reality. The paradox of this percolated understanding is that while it is appreciated by one's psyche, its foundation is experiential and thus defies explanation by Western logic.

The most puzzling experiences many serious visitors have in India (not the touring tourists) are almost impossible to label. They are not outstandingly great nor are they outstandingly unsettling. They are simply experiences that puzzle. We can call them mind adventures.

When we Westerners go to India we face (but rarely acknowledge) two profound influences. I have noted both: the effect of the incredible continuity (weight) of a religious philosophy that has molded a generic mind-set over centuries and very different beliefs about the meaning of life and the nature of man. The predominant Indian belief considers all life has the potentiality for oneness and divinity within, innately, while in contrast, the Western visitor believes his behavior is subordinate to divine commands and heaven is the Kingdom of God. This striking difference means that the individual operates pretty much "out-of-synch" with the culture he is operating in. That is, if you think of a mechanical device that operates by meshing two wheels with cogs, then this is like one wheel with a defective cog that makes its wheel lag behind the first.

I suspect this out-of-synch or non-meshing of ways of perceiving the world sets the stage for the strange happenings that I and many other visitors to India experience.

THE
HOMECOMING

Most of us fortunate enough to live comfortable
though modest lives rarely experience the debilitating poverty
we read about. Sharing the stark realities of true poverty is
never really voluntary nor wholly absolute. Even the happy
hippies of the 60s, who forswore material attachments to live
the communal ashram life usually had the security of home
and family somewhere, ready strings to pull when the novelty
of poverty wore off. The poor in the U.S. and Europe benefit
by welfare programs and social activities. But for the poor of
India there is no such hope, and of the poorest, who live for
generations with not even the prospect of hope, millions upon
millions live in Calcutta.

I did not expect to encounter poverty so intimately
when I first visited my Calcutta friends. Ranjan and Kanak
were husband and wife physicians I had met years before

while they were both on fellowship for advanced medical research at UCLA. In Calcutta each was on the staff of a different medical school, and Kanak had a large, mainly charity, obstetrics practice as well. I had guessed they lived comfortably enough, and in a sense they do. But because India is India and Calcutta is Calcutta, the most dedicated professional helpers of society can remain in India's culture of poverty.

Although afterwards I was to share Ranjan and Kanak's desperately meager existence with scarcely a thought about its physical bareness, the first moments of that first visit to their apartment-cum-clinic (the Victorian preference for a Latin "with" to indicate combinations is a frequent Indian idiom) numbed my mind and spirit with a deeply poignant sadness. After weeks of roaming through India's dusty streets, I was still not prepared to see dear friends rooted in the seamy wanting of poverty.

One of the most profound experiences in my life had been when I first met real poverty. It was long ago, at home, in the decades after the Great Depression before recovery, when poverty was starker, more plaintive, and infinitely more hopeless than it is today when social consciousness is rousing from its long sleep. I became intimate then with the despair of poverty in a brief encounter whose memories have endured as vividly as when they were first impressed upon my mind. I was complying with the senior medical school requirement of delivering babies to slum dwellers. I can still see the beds in corners of one-room tenements or stuffed into closet-sized bedrooms, my eyes straining in the dim lights, using shredded towels for baby blankets, crushing cockroaches doggedly attacking the litter, and resolutely boiling water in rusty tins to bathe the baby.

The cries of sadness that welled in my throat in those dread days surged up my chest again when I saw Kanak's delivery rooms. I had had no preconceived ideas, but I was not prepared for what I saw.

We had driven through the crowded streets of Calcutta, conversation lost in the cacophony of street sounds and car horns, to the final turning down a small dusty side street. We're home, Kanak told me, motioning to her right. But I was staring to the left, across the alleyway where, lined up like small animal sheds, were eight-by-six-foot cubicles where the poor of India struggle to sell their meagre wares, where they live as well, fighting the heat and dirt that seem to fuse their shelters with the steaming, filthy streets. The car had stopped across from the sheds, in front of a gloomy stone structure looking to be some thirty feet wide and about three stories in height.

Kanak screamed, the shrill command of an Amazon mobilizing her troops. Out of the darkness alongside the building came the gate-man, sleepy-eyed, painfully thin, very dark, and with eyes downcast. In a block, Kanak, Ranjan, their small boy Raja, the gate-man and I pushed through the darkness to a faintly lit entrance at the side of the building. Inside, toward the street was a crude storeroom. Some rags and a string cot where the gate-man had been sleeping were all I could see. Ahead were stone steps worn to smooth shallow dishes, and at the entrance to the first level, a torn, faded hanging that no longer hid the doors.

Kanak wanted to show me the "clinic." She shouted upwards to Robie for the keys, and in a moment a slender boy appeared and began to work on the huge padlock. I was to become used to the procedure; every door of the building was the 1880s version of the narrow French double door, and each was padlocked when not in use. In the constant humidity of Calcutta the locks were always rusty and difficult to open; and I got used to that too, waiting for keys to be found, waiting for the locks to yield.

We entered the clinic. For a moment I felt transported into old movie scenes of a medieval warder's office. One faint light bulb, perhaps 10 watts, flickered like a candle over a dark, bulky desk. To the left, through the darkness, blackened iron bars covered the great window that loomed to challenge any entrance from the narrow alleyway outside. There were narrow halls running in both directions from the anteroom. Kanak's sari swished dust clouds as she rushed to the desk, opened a drawer and pulled out her appointment book. She bent over the desk, squinting through her small glasses in the dim light as she read the appointments for the evening. It was nearly eight o'clock and office hours were just beginning.

With her plans set, she ushered me down a dark hallway to a "recovery room." It was a small room with a tiny window looking out to the nowhere of a brick wall next door. In dead center was an iron cot, looking strangely left over from some soldiers' barracks a century ago. I could make out the dark figure of a slim girl lying there with a tiny swaddled baby beside her. The faded blue sliver of canvas ticking barely covered the iron mesh of the cot. At her feet was a dirty small bath towel; above, the usual bare, dim light bulb suspended by a rusty chain from the high ceiling. I kicked embarrassedly as a cockroach crossed my foot.

With a squeal of delight Kanak swept the infant into
her arms. The girl-mother's eyes glowed like burnt amber in
the dim light, and in bursts of Bengali, she and Kanak began
chanting the delights of motherhood and newborn children.
It was almost festive.

Kanak became transformed. Not until then had I
thought that she might have been worried and embarrassed
about the contrast between my life of modest affluence and
hers of desperate poverty. She was an illustrious doctor, on the
faculty of medical schools and hospitals, but there were no
material rewards for her in India. She and Ranjan had clawed
their way through revolutions and poverty to realize their goal
of oneness with the universe, and because their universe was
India, they were, in the best way they could find, being one
with India. Yet Kanak had doubtless worried about how this
ghetto of Indian intellectuals and devotees of spiritual aspirations would appear to her American friend. Then suddenly, as
she rocked the infant in her arms, she became Mother India.
And as Mother India she slipped behind the mirror of another
consciousness.

There are times when you can sense an aura of minds
that live in spiritual places, as being with the right guru or
teacher who shows that spark of the divine. But for those of
us who must stay in the pressing world of cruder spirits, it is
a rare experience to be enveloped in a mood with life and
action that demands our awareness of the cosmic unity. There
was Kanak, the girl-mother and the infant bonded and elevated above darkness into a light one could feel if not see.
They seemed suspended in a space a million miles away in that
evening's duskiness, yet even in the distance they were vibrant

and larger than life. I felt a part of me becoming detached. There was a separation and, painlessly, my Western mores of disgust with dirt and insects, and auras of crude hardships were melted down in a strange non-material warmth. I suddenly realized I was home.

The other rooms of the clinic were darker still, more empty of furniture and more dimly lit, but I was no longer aware of the poverty. They were rooms of joy, rooms of fulfillments, of endings and beginnings. Kanak seemed to grow in stature as she swung into action. It was a sureness of knowing that her years of devoted persevering in the Vedantist conviction that total selflessnes in the service of others was good karma. Earth brown and vigorous, Kanak forgot the contrasts with the United States and was herself again, her Indian self, part of India, part of Mother India. I became taken up in whatever conversion of energy she had just undergone. It was less a matter of becoming unaware of the surroundings, even less a matter of forgetting my own culture than it was of being swept up in an amorphous tide of spirit.

Kanak began doing the things she did every day. We climbed more steps to the second level where the apartment was. The small double doors to the living room were locked and we detoured quite naturally through the dining room that Robie had left unlocked while he attended us below. To the left there was a scuttling of shadows and Kanak departed into them to supervise the preparation of dinner. Ranjan and I settled ourselves in the living room. It was small but seemed larger because of the enormously high ceiling. Here too the bare light bulbs were suspended by long chains from the ceiling. The walls were a curious dirt-brown cream. Toward the street was a closed, draped door and a shut, draped window. Ranjan flicked a wall switch, the bulbous knobby antique kind with an ugly brown toggle switch protruding, and the ceiling fan began to move the air. As an afterthought Ranjan opened the window and cracked the door. Even before that I could hear the street sounds, and with the window and door opened the sounds roared in as if we were in the middle of a street bazaar. I could scarcely hear Ranjan talking.

As we had a bit of tea, I gave Raja the presents I had carried from Los Angeles. It was a shopping bag full, but there are not many fancy or exotic toys you can bring a seven-year-old in a shopping bag across the Pacific in crowded airplanes. But to Raja, I could see immediately, they were treasures from the world he dreamed about but at seven had already given up hope of ever seeing. Not for decades in the United States has there been a reaction like Raja's, not at Christmas parties for the poor or taking the underpriveleged to Disneyland.

Raja was timid, but his expectancy transcended his reticence. He fondled each toy in its wrapper. He opened each with great care, and with infinite tenderness he took each part and each small toy, placed them on the coffee table and patted them with love. It was, in fact, weeks before he would put the whole collection together. Every moment of delight was prolonged. He savored every touch, every sight, every sound of the toys. Then he would put them carefully away to save for the next day.

"Ah," Ranjan began, "show Auntie Barbara your train."

The obedient Raja went to a small shelf, extracted a box, squatted on the floor and put together a small cardboard train set. It was an engine with two paper cars with a track of about a two foot circle. He moved the paper train ever so gently by hand. It was his prize. It was worn with handling but not a scratch showed.

"And show her your zoo."

Raja disappeared into the back shadows of the apartment and reappeared with a small cloth sack. Out of it he tumbled cardboard figures of wild animals. It was his zoo.

> Four years later. . . . "Bring Raja something that is also educational," Kanak had instructed me, and I had brought him a splurge of Viewmaster slides, everything from tours through Africa to comic strips. Raja shrugged. "Oh, I have those," he muttered, and turned to a shining plastic model airplane he had in a box with a score of other plastic models of trucks and cars and rockets. And I kept remembering how difficult it had been to get antibiotics and meat. In four years India had entered the Plastics Age.

But on that first visit, when Raja's rapture was uncontained and happiness was one small toy from America, I was taking in more sights and smells and sounds and meanings than my mind could handle. It is only long afterward that I am wont to make comparisons; my first encounters are always ones of complete absorption into the now, flowing into the reality of what is. And I was hearing street din, loud yet with the comfortable feeling of impersonality one finds in large masses. The sounds, the masses are so sweeping there is no time to set one's self aside as individual or different.

The sounds, the worn tones of the room, the joy of renewing old friendships seemed to carry me instantly into Indian life, and I was home without understanding how home could be where I had never been before, with strange shadows flitting by and darkened rooms I did not understand.

I had seen only two rooms of the apartment, but I had heard a great deal of activity in the dusky shadows so I assumed there might be many rooms. Then I realized there were numerous servants and I began to wonder what they all did and where they all slept. It was only later that I recognized the incongruity. This ancient, small apartment, so meagerly furnished, so dusky dim it reminded me of sharecroppers' huts, this tiny household had five servants.

There was the gate-man whose sole job was to guard the eternally locked entrance, and the driver, whose duty was continuous since Kanak herself went her rounds of hospitals and patients and medical schools almost around the clock, and in the meantime there was Ranjan to be taken to his medical school post, and Raja to be driven to and from school. I had heard that Ranjan had once driven the car, and with the combination of imperious confidence of royal master and his inexperience in driving, the occasion was that of the only accident in his adult life. He never touched a steering wheel again.

Of the other servants, there was the nurse for Raja, a young girl who dressed him but mostly just played with him to keep him contented; and there were the cook and the utility servant who did the washing—a harijan, an untouchable.

They were not simply poor servants, they were servants to the poor. By long custom, poorer relatives or the children of old servants come to serve just to be housed and fed. They may get a few rupees a year, but that is rare. They hover in the background, ears tuned to the call, both content and happy they are not begging in the street.

In following years, I stayed often with the Dasguptas, sharing their lives and poverty and hopes for a better world. I had to watch as India allowed these remarkable sacrificial lambs for human goodness be slaughtered in its environment of inaction and imposed, inappropriate, British-inherited mentality and social values. My dear Kanak, for example, when promoted to full professorship at the medical school, lost 50 percent of her salary—a matter of policy since academic recognition commands higher fees in private practice. When she strained her being to compensate and still reserve half-time for charity work, retinal detachments ended her medical practice.

Ranjan's coping response was the typical romantic Ranjan. The clinic was swept clean, ready for renting, he retired, and the Dasguptas moved to Santiniketan. This was the poet Tagore's place and as well as an idyllic refuge for contemplatives, it also was home to a freethinker's University. Ranjan envisioned Raja's university work there, but alas, Raja had little interest in schooling. He married at sixteen and settled into a routine government job. Nor was Kanak suited for the contemplative countryside. Struggling to provide an income by a wretched train commute to continue her practice in Calcutta, she was felled by a cerebral hemorrhage at the age of fifty-two. Part of my Indian soul died with Kanak.

It can, of course, never be the same again. How well I recall the gathering of medical school professors to demonstrate that levitating one's body could be achieved through proper meditation and yoga. There was Dr. Gupta, a slight but well-built, bronzed figure, working to maintain the lotus position while on the Dasguptas' soft and rumpled bed. The discussion ground on endlessly in the living room and from time to time we would check with Dr. Gupta for his progress. Each time he assured us that levitation was near. By late afternoon most of us were weary with boredom and decided to have tea. A bit later Dr. Gupta sheepishly made his appearance. He simply said he would try again. No one seemed surprised and everyone had faith he would levitate sooner or later. It was all surprisingly matter-of-fact.

I was loath to make a judgment about the group's faith, philosophy or level of technical sophistication. I had had a taste of the latter when I lectured to the graduate medical school and had been grieved by the obvious and painful gap in medical information at one of the better medical institutions in India. I had lectured on new findings in brain physiology and was chided by my audience for "speculation" and not reviewing the subject as it was known. They were, incredibly, using information of twenty years earlier, information now outdated and replaced.

Visits to other medical schools in India made it clear that information interchange was rarely encouraged. The usual route for new medical information to enter India was via visits by Indian academicians to medical congresses in other parts of the world. And much too often, the reports taken home were incomplete or inaccurate.

It taught me not to make comparisons and to accept India on her own terms and at her own pace. And I did enjoy the leisurely discussions at the Lake Club where there was nothing more pretentious or left-over English custom than a servant in a worn-out uniform bringing us our tea on the chigger-filled lawn where we could watch the scullers practice. And I did adore, with a touch of hesitation, Holi day, when

Indians express their friendships by splashing colored water or powdered dye on good friends in honor of Krishna's cavorting way of love, "playing" Holi with the cowherd boys and milkmaids. One "plays" Holi, possibly because the festival arose from old ritual festivals when, once a year, all social, family, and ritual customs were overturned, caste was disregarded and everyone experienced the role of their social opposite. The symbolism of Holi is love, but because it is also an act of devotion, the devotion must be participated in wholly. At times the celebrants abuse the custom, flinging more than the cusomary plastic sacks of colored water, perhaps because social reform of behavior constraints seems so near. Some states have even banned this joyous fesival. Abuse seems to be a world-wide phenomenon.

DADAJI
OF CALCUTTA

It is in Calcutta, the nerve center of Bengal, where a new religious order of Hinduism was formalized around the beginning of this century. Known as Vedanta, the new sect was based on the philosophy of the ancient Vedic writings as interpreted in the Enlightenment of a young monk named Ramakrishna. The new sect rapidly captured much of Calcutta and Bengal and soon found the attention of the intelligentsia throughout the world.

Vedanta's origins are typical of those of most sects in India. After years of extraordinary ascetic devotion to Kali (known in the Hindu hierarchy of deities as the Mother of the Universe, also as the Giver of Life and Death and The Destroyer), and while still at a relatively young age, Ramakrishna was proclaimed as an avatar (an incarnation of a deity) by visiting wise men sometime in the mid-1880s. According to legend, Ramakrishna was mightily surprised but accepted the pronouncement and continued his spiritual explorations.

Although barely able to read or write, the young monk Ramakrishna devoted himself to Vedic scripture and with the intensity of his single-minded concentration on union with the ultimate reality, he developed an unusual skill for interpreting the esoteric Vedas in terms of everyday experience. It was a fitting ability at a time when India was beginning to awaken from a long isolation, and when the metaphysical pronouncements of most other yogic sects invoked the karmic concept that some were born to understand the meaning of the cosmic consciousness while others must content themselves with the worship of deities.

But this was only the first phase of the enlightenment that shaped Vedanta. Ramakrishna's chosen disciples were destined to travel widely and become exposed to the thinking and scientific attitudes of the West. Ultimately Vedanta incorporated a more objective perspective of its philosophy, and it did become more a philosophy and less a religion. Among its departures from traditional yogic thought was its emphasis on social involvement.

And here I was at the Vedanta Centre.

Hamijin tapped softly at my dormitory door, opened it and slid the coffee tray on the desk noiselessly.

"Good morning," I managed as I pushed the sheet aside and sat up in bed. Hamijin grinned, happy that a guest was not only awake when he brought morning coffee, but was not meditating and had a moment to exchange greetings.

I was in the dormitory of the Vedanta Study Centre, and of all life's luxuries, this spartan hostel afforded the greatest—bed coffee. In my travels through India, I tend to avoid hotels catering to Westerners, and although most strictly Indian hotels leave much to be desired, I can excuse all their faults knowing I can wake up to the superb coffee of India. Even here in the austere quarters of the Vedanta Centre, steaming bed coffee was served just for the asking.

Showered and dressed, I spent a long time absorbing the tiny fragments of Indian life unfolding as I watched through the giant window of my room or from the balcony outside the door that overlooked the inner courtyard. Looking down I could see the ashram coming to life in the delicious early morning air. And from the window I could see across the narrow street to a city jungle known only to India. There, in worn splendor, were the remnants of a large colonial mansion. Parts of the third floor porch roof were missing; most of the windows had no glass at all; rubble filled the areas to the sides; stairways were dangerously decayed. Still, one could see bits of material made into an awning, and along one porchway hung a dingy laundry. I watched as shadowy figures moved about inside.

To the left, in what had no doubt once been a garden, was an open stone shed and the shambled remains of a wooden horse stall, both barely surviving the weedy overgrowth. A man and young boy walked toward the stone shed. There they opened the water tap and began a grand ritual of cleansing. From top to bottom they washed and scrubbed with joy and ritual intensity. They would be clean! As usual, they scrubbed and rinsed with underpants on, much used to public bathing. Satisfied, they then performed their tooth brushing rituals.

These were the dirty Indians the tourists complain about? Indeed! I suppose pink-white Westerners cannot understand that coffee-brown skin need not turn white to be clean! Except for religious pilgrims dusty after a long day's march or an intentionally encrusted beggar, I have never seen an unclean Indian. I wondered how many Westerners could live in such poverty and be so clean.

The courtyard of the ashram, too, was beginning a new day. A few straggler cooks, bearers and sweepers moved silently through the back gateway, a stone arch with a massive iron gate that could be closed to seal off the city noise. It was always difficult for me to use one entrance over the other. I loved them both. Here in the back of the courtyard was the small street where cars could travel and where I met the Dasguptas' car or began my walk to their apartment. To the front of the courtyard was the magnificent lobby of the Vedanta Study Centre, a high vaulted entryway, much like, I guessed, those of centuries-old British university libraries. It was done in elegant rose and grey marble with a semi-colonnade. Off to the right was the entrance to the Vedantists' library, quite possibly one of the best, most modern libraries in all of India. This morning I could see a foreign scholar begin his walk to the dining room, hoping for an early breakfast. It was intensely quiet and still. A few scattered rosebushes spoke of the garden hopes for the Centre.

The boundaries of my being melted into the utter dispassion of the scenes my mind absorbed. Outside, I knew, was the turmoil of Calcutta, storms of people-sounds, car horns, the thuds of trolleys and hand-drawn carts bumping over the paving blocks, yet here, within the city ashram walls, all was a calm island of repose where one's being could flow into the spirit of the cosmos. I marveled at the power of the place, the power of healing and nurturing the spirit without a guru or a congregation anywhere in sight. If I were to speak of this experience of spirit to colleagues at home, I would be assured that my childish mind had created this idyllic state from my emotional wishbook.

I was reluctant to leave this unique contemplation but a new adventure lay ahead. After days of coaxing and cajoling, Ranjan had finally agreed to take me to one of Calcutta's few resident swamis. Ranjan was every bit as much a skeptic of the spiritual and mystic as he had been a political revolutionary and he was adamant that I should not waste time with religious charlatans. Pleading it was necessary to my research, I finally persuaded him to take me to the only local guru he could locate.

Calcutta does not abound in practitioners of the occult nor in wonder-working holy men. The Bengali temperment inclines more toward Western notions of the intellectual, regarding its approach to spirituality as enlightened and rational. The philosophers of India agree, and particularly in the Bengal where Vedanta was born, that possession of magical powers (the siddhis) is a mark of spirituality only when such powers are used solely and most discriminately as an aid to achieve full realization. No one in India denies such powers exist or that they cannot be within the reach of anyone who wishes them. Yet nowhere in India do spiritual communities admit that true saddhus, the Enlightened Ones, ever willfully display their psychic powers. It is, in fact, characteristic of Hindu doctrine to explain the existence of siddhis in a bewildering profusion of contradictions. Siddhis can be learned but one does not seek them. It is only by the practice of single-minded meditation on the Ultimate Reality that the powers develop, not when the goal of meditation is to gain the powers. The powers that can change air to gold, move buildings, that can transport the self beyond the world, that can read and direct the thoughts of others, all these powers are mere extensions of our normal abilities to affect what we encounter every day. Once possessed, the powers are not to be used; they are the by-products of purity of heart. Most intellectuals, especially in Bengal, accept this rule of spiritual achievement as did my intellectual, activist, skeptical friend Ranjan.

Ranjan and the car were at the gate by nine. Ranjan was strangely objective about visiting the swami this morning, and I soon discovered he was reluctantly reconsidering his judgment about the swami since he had just learned that a former political ally was a devotee. The guru's name was Dadaji, Ranjan said.

Now anyone who knows India at all knows that *every* swami's name is either Dadaji or Babaji or Dada or Baba— or sometimes, if female, Mati. Some philosophic theorists have opined that the tight family structure and father authority tradition of India allowed sons no place to escape to *except* an ashram. So one supposes that calling the chief swami or one's guru Baba (somewhat equivalent to our Daddy) or Dada (older brother) came naturally.

In any event, this particular Dadaji (the suffix ji indicates special affection and respect), lived a long way out in the suburbs of Calcutta. We crossed the Hoogly river, famous for the hordes of white dhoti'd workers that cross it twice a day to and from work and connecting trolleys, and finally travelling into what looked like lower density neighborhoods. Not that there are single houses, but the apartments are more often two than three storied. Finally we turned down a narrow street. It was lined with open gutters along each side but there were stone blocks at each building to cross the gutter. Each building also had a small fence with entrance gate.

We found Dadaji's house and at Ranjan's tap, a pretty young girl in a strangely hippy type of sari let us in and ushered us up the stairs to a small bookshelf-lined bedroom on the second floor. Here she gave us an introductory speech then displayed several full-page newspaper articles about Dadaji.

"India's Miracle Man Proclaims Krishnamurti" one headline screamed. I knew Krishnamurti's philosophy and his integrity and I was surprised he would render any testimonial about personal psychic powers. Another newspaper heralded Dadaji as India's greatest guru and was crammed with blocks of stories about the many miracles he had wrought. The pretty young girl appeared to be both a secretary and PR agent. Finally she asked our names and wrote them down on small business-like cards in red ink with a fine scrawl. I wondered what that was for (it turned out to be part of a "miracle"). At last we were ready to be shown in to Dadaji, the great guru himself.

I shall never forget the scene. Incongruous to my Western eyes, there on a long mahogany couch lay Dadaji in the resting Buddha position. The couch itself was long and one could see immediately that Dadaji was very tall, at least six feet six. He was in repose, apparently just ending meditation, elbow folded, and head resting on his hand, with his great brown eyes open but not focusing.

On the shining hardwood floor were some dozen devotees sitting in half-yoga postures or with legs drawn up in relaxed sitting. There was Ranjan's former political friend, and, in a hushed introduction by the secretary, another political leader and member of the Parliament, two physicians, some business leaders and a scattering of housewives. Quite an elite following, I thought.

It was noontime, the devotees gathering here on their lunch break. No one had much time to spare, so everyone quieted quickly and Dadaji began his discourse (gurus discourse, they never lecture or just give a talk). Dadaji's message was that no one needs a guru because every person is his own guru.

To most Indians and certainly to most Westerners charmed by Hindu philosophy, Dadaji's discourses on being one's own guru would seem heresy. One of the pop words of the 70s' spiritual searching youth, and even today, is "guru." Almost everywhere in India saddhus and swamis caution that spiritual progress is impossible without a guru.

The concept of guru is universal. Throughout history seekers of knowledge have recognized the need for a teacher. But in India, with its philosophy of experiential wisdom, it is the selection of the guru that raises questions in the Western intellectual mind. In Indian tradition there are few ways in which guru and seeker enter into a relationship. Usually, the seeker of realization visits ashrams where well-known gurus hold audience for their devotees. At times the guru of a particular ashram will answer questions or solve spiritual problems for a seeker in a way that sparks instant rapport between the two. The guru is convinced of the sincerity of the seeker and the seeker becomes intuitively aware of the spiritual wisdom of the guru. It is settled. Once this chemistry between the two has been recognized, the relationship is established for eternity. The guru remains the teacher even after his death. Of course if the chemistry does not happen, the guru does not accept the seeker as his pupil and the seeker continues his search.

Some seekers find this apparently indiscriminate, chancy selection of a teacher for all life and the thereafter highly suspect in its procedure. The analytically inclined want evidence to prove a particular saddhu really does understand both philosophy and the real world. There are many learned, well-educated gurus and there are, as well, many unlearned, uneducated gurus who appear to possess, instead, intuitive knowledge. The cautious, the skeptic, and the indoctrinated scientist often have difficulty accepting intuitive knowledge over traditionally learned knowledge.

When a guru tells me there is a blue pearl of wisdom within the recesses of my brain that is the source of all brain activity (as Swami Mukdananda once told me), I am fairly sure he doesn't mean there is a *real* pearl there. But if that is so, why does he say "blue"? On the other hand, if I accept the blue pearl as a symbol of spiritual energy and source of wisdom, then my analytic nature must contend with the problem of how that energy is converted into an energy that can move brain neurones and guide them to direct my thoughts and behavior.

Still, many intellectual seekers, including some scientists, have no difficulty at all with the guru concept. Two such scientists described their experiences with Dadaji in *The Illus-trated Weekly of India* (March 19, 1978). One was Dr. R.L. Datta, President of the International Solar Energy Society and writer of the article, while the other was Dr. William Klein, President of the Smithsonian Biological Radiation Institute of Washington, D.C., who was also accompanied by his wife. They were all witness to a succession of manifestations of objects and writing Dadaji materialized from out of nowhere. The printing on watches and watchbands disappeared and was replaced by writing dictated by Dr. Klein's thoughts; a golden locket became suspended from a neck chain; Dadaji's name was written on paper while Dadaji was across the room.

While the article extols the miraculous ability of Dadaji to transcend physical nature by thought alone, to be fair to Dr. Klein, this adoring praise appears to be Dr. Datta's, not Dr. Klein's. Dr. Datta apparently became a devotee and was with Dadaji many times. Nowhere in the lengthy article is there any endorsement by Dr. Klein. Dr. Datta's article is entitled "Conversion of a Scientist" and ends with a long and glowing tribute to the spiritual power of Dadaji. One surprising quote from Dadaji is, "A human being can never be a guru."

But here Dadaji was lecturing on and on in Bengali, far too long at any one time to allow for proper translation as Ranjan was trying to do for me. The long periods of Bengali gave me an opportunity to reflect on the entire episode. Here was Dadaji saying that you do not need a guru, you are the guru. Yet here were his devotees, kneeling before him, and what were they if not devotees and pupils, and he their guru?

After a short meditation, the devotions were over. The secretary reappeared and led me back into the other bedroom while the devotees left and Ranjan went down to wait in his car. In an almost conspiritorial tone the secretary asked if I would like to have Dadaji perform a miracle for me. Of course! Who wouldn't want to have a miracle done especially for them?

I was led into still another room. There was Dadaji in a yoga meditation position on a pillow, a cloth spread in front of him and another pillow opposite him (for me), with a slightly elevated altar to the side between us. The secretary explained that Dadaji would first cause my name to be written without touching the paper. He showed me a small card-sized white piece of paper, turned it over and over to show that it was blank, then took it and put both hands behind his back. He muttered a few words, a bit like chanting, drew his arms in front and deposited a white paper in front of me. The girl said to turn it over, and there, sure enough, was my name, written in red ink in a fine scrawl!

Next, the secretary said, Dadaji would make a gift for me. This time I would need to close my eyes and say a mantra that Dadaji gave me. I said the mantra, opened my eyes and Dadaji waved another small white paper in front of me. This time it was a short mantra. Dadaji said this second mantra was secret, mine alone, and when said it would have great power. Then for the gift. I was to close my eyes, say the new mantra over and over until Dadaji told me to open my eyes. Of course I peeked and watched surreptitiously while Dadaji worked frantically with both arms behind his back. Finally he told me to look. He brought his hands to the front, opened his closed fists and placed a huge ball of brown gooey candy in front of me. I had watched the whole thing and rated Dadaji as one of the worst magicians of all time. A twelve-year-old could have done better.

With considerable awe, not for Dadaji, but in profound puzzlement over why intelligent devotees could accept this man as a spiritual teacher, I went down the steps in a daze, out to Ranjan and the car. I had completely forgotten to make a contribution to Dadaji, mainly, I suppose, because I felt it would be paying for a performance that was too awful to pay for.

I looked around. Dadaji was coming after us. He wanted me to have some booklets. Ranjan, anxious to escape, offered to pay for them but Dadaji shook him off saying they were a gift and went back into his house. The booklets contained scores of testimonials to Dadaji's powers (the siddhis). Here is the testimony of Sachin Roy Chowdbury, L.L.B., F.A.C. (London), Chartered Accountant:

> "Dada is not guru but is possessor of the AB-SOLUTE TRUTH . . . and (this) vests him with any and every power that the Almighty can have. At His will so many unheard of or unthinkable objects can be created and controlled by Dada. So we witness . . . Dada is offering a woollen shawl from the atmosphere to Dr. Gopinath Kaviraji in Benares, his name being embroidered at the corner with the help of Dada's thumb. Again, by a touch on the forehead of Mr. Jain, Chief Engineer, Utter Pradesh, a miniature photo of Sri Satyanarain was embossed there. . . . remaining there for more than three days as was witnessed by several thousands of people. . . . Dada is omnipresent and whenever I longed for him, he did appear with that sweet scented fragrance. At the time Dada was present with me, he was also present with my wife at Calcutta.
> And from Professor Arabinda Bhattacharya: "Whatever (Dadaji) touches emits a wonderful odour. Tea becomes wine and wine turns into milk.

From airy nothing Dadaji produes sweets, medicine
or pictures of Ram." Paradoxically, the professor
continues that gurus are only "mortal men who
make a show of their prowess to produce God gift-
packed, as and when desired. Their unassuming,
God-fearing superstition-ridden disciples gaze in
wonder, listen to their lectures and return home convinced that their Gurus are holding all the tickets to
salvation. Dada always advises people to keep clear
of such religious fakes."

And Dr. Anjali Mukherjee, M.B.B.S.,
D. Obst; R.C.O.G. (London); Dr. C.O.G.;
M.R.C.O.G. (London), Consulting Gynaecologist,
describing her experience when Dadaji gave her a
mantra, says, "Suddenly I heard some whispers in
the name of God three times. The Mahanam entered
through my ears and then circulated in my brain and
reached my heart and stopped there. My whole body
became still for a few moments and tears flew in my
eyes. When Dada asked me to read the contents of
the paper in my hands, I realized, before I read
(what) Mahanam written on the paper by invisible
hands, that the Nam had already entered in my
heart. It was really the Red-Letter Day for me."

The worst was yet to come. It was nearly two years
before I returned to Calcutta. One of my first questions was
whether Ranjan had ever heard again about Dadaji. Indeed he
had and had the newspaper clippings to prove it.

Dadaji was languishing in jail, arrested and convicted
for two serious crimes. One conviction was for tampering with
wills. Apparently he had persuaded his wealthy devotees to
give him their wills for safe-keeping and then did a bit of
forgery that left all real money to Dadaji. The conviction for
the second crime put Dadaji away for some time. He was

found guilty of white slavery, of importing young girls from rural areas to sell into prostitution.

Ranjan kept saying, "I told you so."

In September, 1986, I discovered Dadaji lecturing in Los Angeles.

ANIRVAN

I've often said, "Drop a syllable to an Indian and he'll talk for a week." And so it always was with my friend Ranjan, he of the Indian Revolution, the philosopher, and the only sometimes medical school professor. I remember when the Medical College kicked him upstairs as a token, I guessed, of their respect for him as one of the true political activists that had brought India its liberation. The visions that made Ranjan a crusader for liberty and freedom also made him a dreamer in the world of science. He had taxed even Indian patience and finally someone else was named to head his department while he was moved to a semi-honorary position. The change fit him for Ranjan was also, paradoxically, a true patrician, and reveled in his new role as senior educator and honorary chief of graduate medical education. The trouble was, his dreams were ever so much brighter than the reality of Calcutta could offer. He was fortunate that his wife, Kanak, was not only brilliant and energetic, but was also wholly devoted to his well-being. Otherwise, I'm sure Ranjan would have found his security in a political prison or any place where he could expound and discourse and debate without worrying about making a living. It seemed that for Ranjan time had stood still until the day he discovered the poet Tagore. Ever after he would seek refuge in the dreams for a civil world that recognized human worth, the dreams he shared with Tagore.

Living with Ranjan and Kanak, I also began to realize why philosophy and religion fill so much of Indian life. First, one has to remember that the West raped the labor and land of India for a very long time until British commerce finally conquered it all. Few native Indians, save for small colonies of Parsees in Bombay and Gujarat state, along with a pocket or two of Imperial Moslims Nawobs (as in Hyderabad) and the Portuguese Catholic colony of Goa, were able to compete against the commercial efficiency of the West. Indians became slaves, servants, underlings, puppets and hostages in their own land. Without any way to compete commercially, without a military or a spirit for fighting, and lacking the Western forms and logic of communication, Indians reacted according to their value system that this was their karma and that ultimately the conditions of life would change as they always do, even if the change took millennia.

In most of India, as recently as a decade ago, life for the average Indian (regardless of caste) had no escape from the strictures on life imposed by the need to adapt to British customs as a way to survive her imperial rule. I recoiled in anger and pain, for instance, when my friends first toured me around Calcutta. Except for the Grand Hotel and Chowringhee Road, both of which were undergoing a desultory reconstruction, the city seemed separated into two parts, the people of India and their daily survival activities in one compartment and scores of great monuments to British heroes, enormous playgrounds for cricket and soccer and a giant racecourse, and elaborate, ungodly wide avenues in another compartment. Thousands of Indians drain their energies daily as they cross and criss-cross the expanded avenues a hundred times in the course of a day's work, avenues made for British armies to parade upon. And I listened as Ranjan and Kanak told of the decades of injustice India had suffered, the infamy of the Black Hole of Calcutta and scores of sickening abuses of Indian lives by the British occupiers. Yet when I questioned Ranjan why the giant Victoria monument remained as such a prominent landmark, his patrician heritage (real or assumed) reminded me that one should remember people who had made historic impacts and that both the famous and infamous had a place in the human hierarchy. He admitted that the monument had a good many scars inflicted by unthoughtful radicals that he truly abhored, and I was duly impressed by his very Indian attitude of tolerance and nonviolence.

Most Indian cities abound in massive concrete remnants of British colonialism, monoliths made for the grandeur of British rule and commerce, but so clearly inappropriate to Indian needs and way of life. Still today in Calcutta, Delhi and Bombay, for example, bearers rush by train or foot to take their masters hot meals at noontime. There are no cooking rooms in the leftover office buildings, no places for restaurants nearby. The British, of course, had their clubs, but these were rarely open to Indians.

So part of the daily life of the average Indian is spent coping with the obstacles to living and cultural remnants an earlier era made for foreign pleasure. The effort needed to survive is staggering. To work means to travel to work, and whether by trolley or private car, the streets are dirty, unrepaired, noisy, awash with stifling heat and incredibly distant from anyone's home. Worse, a workday can be twelve hours and a workweek can be seven days. There is little leisure time, and there are few options for any free time that might exist. Indian movies occupy a special place in Indian society. Until nearly 1984, Indian movies were 99 percent fantasy films— adventure, life in regal India, steamy love stories that attract the uneducated much more than the educated, yet everyone in India seems to be very knowledgeable about Indian movies.

For most average Indians there is little social life. Television arrived only recently and is state controlled, so you know what that's like. Most adults have a late dinner (by circumstance), have a chat and are off to bed. Some of the more fortunate join clubs, everything from the Jockey Club or the Cricket Club to my friend's Lake Club. At the Lake Club we could sit on the lawn and have tea and watch the scullers practice rowing laps around the lake and waterways.

The principal recreation is what I call "meeting with a purpose." And while Indians do indeed just have parties from time to time, mainly, just like Westerners, groups meet to talk about common interests. There is a marvelous difference, however. Indian soirees are mostly formally arranged, from time of arrival to time of leaving. Everyone is an honored visitor. Guests are usually seated around the perimeter of the room, leaving the center empty as if there were going to be dancing or entertainment. For meetings with a mission, the hosts start a conversation by asking a question. The answer is usually a soliloquy, and other speakers follow in turn. I have been at such gatherings when a diversity of religious, swamis and priests, really went at it in some fits of temper and I felt that the formal seating arrangement helped considerably to avoid a physical confrontation.

The most relaxed social events are either weddings or celebrations of specific events, such as birthdays or receptions for a special visitor. Even for the latter, seating typically begins with guests lining the room perimeter, and the purpose of the party is a little bit like "show and tell." Each guest is asked to sing or recite, and the guest usually obliges with a selection that represents his or her home region. It has always puzzled me why this form of home entertainment is traditional nearly everywhere in the world except in the United States. In the Appalachians and occasionally in other regions, the custom of individual perfomance can be found but it is not widely practiced.

With such limited time and so few diversions except working to survive, it is small wonder so many Indians become absorbed in examining their philosophies of life. On the other hand, a number of archeological finds indicate that by at least 3000 B.C. the early inhabitants of India seriously practiced discipline of mind and body and observed their doctrines of peace (villages and cities had no apparent defenses). It seems likely that the dominance of spiritual influences in daily life that is so prominent in India today is not solely an act of preserving Indian traditions, but in a land so long isolated and insulated from the material revolutions of the West, the focus on religious philosophies is both spiritually nourishing and a national security blanket.

I was fascinated but also a little restless whenever the Dasguptas shared one of their social evenings with me. The invited was always a small circle of friends from the medical schools and one or more swamis from the Vedanta Centre. Westerners must remember that the national conviction of India is that health of being depends upon the yogic discipline of mind and body. From this perspective it is completely natural for the Indian physician to be concerned with philosophy and the insights philosophy can provide into the nature of man through learning to understand the unity and harmony of the universe.

Once during such a philosophic discussion Ranjan mentioned the name Anirvan and he did so with such great reverence, I was immediately intrigued.

"Who is this Anirvan?" I asked after the guests left.

Ranjan sank back into his chair, pulled his body together as if preparing for an assault, looked down at his feet and muttered. It was most uncharacteristic of the imperious Ranjan.

"He. . . . a Sanscrit scholar." I could scarcely hear him.

It was obvious that something was bothering Ranjan. I did not want to pursue a topic that might be sensitive for him, yet there was such a great discrepancy between his faltering behavior and his usual obvious enthusiasm for both Sanscrit and scholars that I knew something was disturbing him. I knew, too, that if he were talking about Tagore, he would literally be acting out his ardor for his hero. I began to probe, carefully.

Finally Ranjan told me that Shri Anirvan was a renowned scholar and guru, a revered intellectual and philosopher and he admitted that he held Anirvan in such high esteem that he worried I would reject discussion of him because he was not the kind of swami or mystic I was hunting. I reminded

Ranjan that I had always been in awe of the extraordinary insights of the philosophers of pre-Christian eras whose wisdom is preserved in Sanscrit. And I argued that I would cherish meeting such a scholar a good bit more than chasing down suspect gurus and swamis. I was especially enchanted to learn that Anirvan's name means "one who always shines, is never extinguished." It was a shock when Ranjan revealed that Anirvan lived nearby. I immediately began to beg Ranjan to take me to him.

Ranjan advised me that Anirvan had been in failing health for several years and that he was not expected to live the month out. Still, he would see what he could do.

Incredibly, Anirvan granted me an interview. It was the philosophic highlight of my life, just as my second visit to him was the occasion of enormous pain.

Ranjan and I walked the few blocks to the apartment house where Anirvan lived. The apartments were typical, "middle class," vast chains of apartment houses endlessly lining the narrow streets angled into each other at unexpected junctures. We entered the apartment, removed our shoes and walked up the steps to the third floor where a young girl took charge and led us into a bedroom. Rough wooden bookshelves lined two of the walls while a third gave onto broad open windows where soft light filtered in through gauze curtains. A three-quarter size low wooden bed filled the fourth side of the room, and there, lying upon pure white sheets lay the smallest figure of a man I have ever seen. He looked to be well into his eighties, no more than five feet, and so painfully thin I would guess he weighed no more than 70 pounds. He was pale, very pale, and his small head with its snowy white hair was sunk into a fluffy white pillow. I was surprised that there was no odor of illness at all; instead, the entire house had the smell of laundry freshened in fast flowing mountain streams.

Ranjan whispered an introduction. Anirvan spoke. His voice was so weak and the effort to speak so great that I despaired of ever hearing his words. Ranjan told me to put my head down to his face. As I did, I asked and received permission to use my tiny tape recorder. I asked Anirvan if he favored any special philosophic guides in the search for enlightenment. In a voice so faint and feeble it scarcely registered on the tape recorder, Anirvan said that each person must look unto himself and work to achieve intelligent understanding of the events and influences in life. I asked about how ordinary people, not spiritual recluses, could achieve enlightenment and how he could tolerate the spiritual charlatans, and what one would do if enlightenment really ever did come.

He said, briefly, to keep an active mind, to pursue understanding by continued query, never to be satisfied with answers. He said also to understand the despair and spiritual poverty of pretenders to spiritual guruship and offer them understanding. And finally, he told me that if enlightenment came, it would also bring with it the knowledge of what it means to living and the life of the spirit.

Anirvan's responses were "condensed." That is, each sentence embraced such breadth and depth of meaning it would be unfair and negligent to give a literal account of our meeting. I can only report that I was enveloped in an aura of love and vision and a momentary immediacy of knowing. It was as if Anirvan were surrounded by a halo. He wasn't, of course, but I did feel as if the spirit of the Absolute had spoken. I could understand Ranjan's reticence and concern about exposing Anirvan to possible misunderstanding.

I have never really recovered from the awe I felt. Some years later I read the account Lizelle Reymond wrote about her five years with Anirvan (*To Live Within,* Doubleday, 1971). At the end of this section I have appended an excerpt from her book as she quotes Anirvan's answer to the question, "What is the function of the interiorization of consciousness?" You can immediately feel the extraordinary intellectual-spiritual level of Anirvan's enlightenment. If ever one has contemplated deeply the meanings of life, one moment with Anirvan could be worth a decade of contemplation.

I felt so strongly about the remarkable gifts of Anirvan that I prayed he was still alive when my UCLA tour group arrived in Calcutta some two years later. Remarkably he was, and I and my group were granted a short visit. Again I mounted the stairs to the third floor, but this time the group and I were shown into a room used as a reception hall. Two visitors were just leaving, and I marveled at Anirvan's endurance and how freely he gave of his disappearing reservoir of strength. We were led into his bedroom and there he was, looking exactly as I had seen him two years earlier. Graciously he said he remembered me. Several of the group began to hover over him with giant tape recorders and shouting questions. I was a bit taken aback, and finally the attending family member said it was time to go.

We wound our way down the stairs onto the street where our bus waited. I was eager to learn how Anirvan had affected the group. Strangely, there seemed to be no reactions,

but as I turned to get some straggling members onto the bus,
I heard one of the women say,

"The nerve of her! Taking us to see that dirty old
man!"

Back in my hotel room I cried. I felt that I had betrayed
Anirvan, that I should have been more knowing about the
spiritual maturity of members of the tour group. I realized,
too, that I had failed to convey understanding about the depth
and grandeur of the mental and spiritual treasures of India.

Epilogue

The UCLA tour group was an absolutely incredible
collection of strange people. Because of libel laws, I cannot
detail the many untoward incidents that occurred with them
while we were in India. Suffice it to say that my emotions were
shredded daily and I was in a constant struggle with the idea
that I had betrayed all of India, her people, her history and her
heritage. Most of us did not part happily.

Then, nearly three years after the tour, I received an
invitation to come to a reunion of the tour group (first reunion, the invitation noted), and to bring whatever pictures I
might have. I had a dozen albums of pictures and the pleasure
of showing them outweighed the store of suppressed, unpleas-
ant memories. I decided to go.

The reunion brought out every one of the insensitive,
boorish members. I steeled myself against more cruel and
disparaging remarks about India and my dear Indian friends.
Astoundingly I was greeted with genuine affection, and all
afternoon I heard remarks such as,

"Wasn't that the most incredible trip!"

"I never learned so much in my life."

"I didn't realize how little I knew until that trip."

"It was the greatest experience of my life."

"I wish I could go back—with the group."

"I feel so close to India."

"I tell everyone that my mind was born on that trip."

"I'll never forget meeting that great man, Anirvan."

And for the first time in three years, I felt at peace. India had been victorious once more. I should have known that few are immune to India's mysterious power to move minds.

From:

To Live Within, The story of five years with a Himalayan guru, Lizelle Reymond, George Allen & Unwin Ltd., London, 1972. Translated from the French. First published by Doubleday & Company, 1971.

At a "class", Shri Anirvan had put the following question: "What is the function of the interiorization of consciousness?"

"It . . . becomes a question. . . . of a deepening and widening of consciousness, which is the aim of spirituality. There is no divorce between the aim of spirituality and the aim of life, which is growth. Spiritual search is a conscious effort to grow by harmonious assimilation and at the same time an intensification of consciousness.

"But how many steps to climb! As soon as we have set out on our way, we try to spiritualize every instant of our life in a conscious or unconscious manner. Should the unconscious effort be supported by favorable social conditions or by a rudimentary inner

need, it is already a preparation for a conscious
effort, for the entire process depends on the dyna-
mism of consciousness in search of clarity. Indeed, a
sort of clarity comes as soon as the sensory values of
animal life begin to be transformed into values of the
understanding. The power to handle ideas is a con-
quest of consciousness. But though sensations may
be clear and precise, the way they are understood by
one person and another are very different. Sensations, even badly interpreted, are the only instru-
ment a man possesses at the beginning of his search
to put an order into his experiences, to shape his way
of life, and to discover the laws of Great Nature.

". . . . Such is the pivot on which the spiritual
effort turns: to transform the given values to the
point where consciousness becomes dynamically free
in its enjoyment of the 'I'. It is here that the interiorization of consciousness comes into play. This is the
inescapable first step to be made. One of the rishis
of the Upanishads clearly formulated its law: 'Pure
Existencse (Sat) pierces an opening to project itself
into the phenomenal world.' Human consciousness
obeys the same law, but the result is a degredation
and a blunting of the conscious energy. To maintain
the fire of life within it, the process has to be re-
versed.

And Shri Anirvan said further:

"If formulated in an abstract way, the call to
observe oneself seems fantastic and even alarming at
the beginning, yet to look into the depths of oneself
is a necessary stage in the evolution of consciousness.
Since it is an aim to be pursued in everyday life, the
way of going about it must be clear and all the pos-
sibilities foreseen. What is more, it must be known
that a certain quality of imagination will necessarily
be utilized by the thought. In other words, it is necessary to 'imagine' what pure thought will be and to
know at the same time that pure thought will only

arise when the habitual automatism of thought is suspended. The same applies to our life, when in the midst of our preoccupations, a temporary and voluntary suspension of all activity is necessary to clarify our consciousness. Even if that moment is very short, consciousness will discern, in a flash of perception, what comes from the outer world and what from the inner world. But to exert any control whatsoever, one must first of all be able to control one's own thoughts. Therefore a control dictated from outside —let us call it a voluntary discipline—must play a role until the inner being is revealed."

YOGA
TRADITIONS

Like most people, I have had difficulties trying to un-
scramble the incredibly tangled skeins of Indian philosophy,
a task I pursued in my quest to understand the mind of
India.

India is one of the few nations of the world whose
evolution has been continuously shaped by the philosophic
beliefs of its people rather than by politics or the competition
of commerce or the internal warring that shapes other nations
of the world. This does not mean that India's history and
beliefs are any less complex. Hindu philosophy is, in fact, a
mosaic of a hundred ways the Indians of prehistory defined the
goals of life, a system of philosophy that gradually became the
Vedas, the sacred texts of Hindus, as Aryan tribes moved
down Persia and across the Indus Valley more than three
thousand years ago.

It is unclear in Indian annals precisely how and when the Vedas arose. It is generously agreed among historians that the four books and 208 verses of the Rig-Veda were accumulated between 1000 and 600 B.C., although some sources believe they were developed as early as 6000 to 2500 B.C., and represented an amalgam of the views of life by the original inhabitants, presumably the Dravidians (the dark-skinned), along with observations and interpretations of the intensely polytheistic religion of tribes of Aryan (the light-skinned) invaders. By 100 A.D. a great library of philosophic works had already been created. The major works of this era that describe the Hindu philosophic tradition are listed at the end of this section.

The surprising mix of philosophy, myth, and history of sacred Hindu works only partly accounts for the complexity and apparent inconsistency of authoritative descriptions of Hindu philosophy. After studying scores of texts on the history and philosophy of India, I could see at least three powerful reasons for the snarl that surrounds accounts of Indian philosphy and history: (1) the very different way Indian sages organize and structure knowledge compared to the way the West processes its information (the Hindu structure knowledge experientially in contrast to structuring it according to the logic of Western science); (2) the voluminous elaboration on the organization and structure of the psyche, and of mind and consciousness, along with endless lists that classify every path and procedure in every Indian philosophic system; and (3) the historical social organization of how stages of life are to be lived, with each directed toward individual union with the ultimate reality.

The first reason (noted above) for the general inatten-
tion to Indian religious philosophy seems to come from the
way Westerners *perceive* philosophic testaments, for what you
begin to realize is that the structure of Indian belief systems
is fundamentally different from the way beliefs are structured
in the West. We Westerners have followed the scientific
model since long before science developed it. That is, we want
to see conclusions (truths) supported by convincing evidence
and by logical argument—*our* system of logic. (That propen-
sity is, in fact, how modern Westerners came to accept articles
of faith as just as good evidence as physical data—ask any
Fundamentalist or Federalist or Catholic.) The scientific
model Westerners hold as the ultimate test of a truth, however, rejects nearly all experiential data (except for their own
religious beliefs), creating a belief system that makes it difficult
for Westerners to even look at Hindu thought without
prejudice.

In contrast, the most ancient of Indian philosophic concepts, *particularly* those based on experiential reports about
the inner mind and consciousness, are treated as sacred, indis-
putable evidence for the validity of Hindu philosophy. When
this reverence for truths derived from inner, contemplative
experience is combined with the Hindu emphasis on the *individual* searching for identity with the universal reality, the
philosophic doctrines are stretched to include a thousand
variations on the original theme. There are, for example,
scores of ways of identifying kinds of stages of yoga, scores of
different mind and body disciplines for every kind of spiritual
journey, and a hundred kinds and divisions of man's interior
senses. Of these, enough substantial analyses of Hindu beliefs

have survived to be both believable and confusing to the Westerner whose model allows only one truth about anything. Thankfully, modern Western historians agree well enough to be able to give a reasonable picture of how the people of India express their philosophic beliefs in the conduct of their lives.

One's conduct in life is, in fact, the fundamental pillar of the Hindu belief system. Dharma means both the way one conducts one's self in life as well as the pursuit of good for all. It is also often interpreted as religious service to perform the duties that pertain to one's station in life. Although it is a universal obligation to pursue the reality, dharma is a very flexible concept and allows each seeker a way to spiritual fulfillment according to conditions and one's means.

According to Indian (Hindu) philosophic tradition there are four stages in life's journey for spiritual fulfillment. These stages are called asramas which means rest-places and also means training grounds. The four asramas are:

Brahmacharya, the period of studentship when the student goes to live with his teacher, studies, refrains from pleasures, and communes with nature, then returns home.

Garhastha, the stage of the householder. Marriage is considered a sacrament and individuals should respect the obligations of marriage. One important social advantage of this stage is that it provides support for those who are engaged in the other stages of life's spiritual journey.

Vanaprastha, the stage of the ascetic, when the obligations of marriage have been fulfilled, the individual should then seek ways to increase spiritual growth. This stage involves several periods designed as preparation for the final stage.

Sannyasa, the life of renunciation, the stage when all worldly cares are renounced in order to achieve the supreme goal of moksa, liberation. The days are spent in contemplation and working to achieve perfection.

There are, of course, different ways for achieving perfection of spirit. We generally know these as the different kinds of yoga. The three best known are:

Karma-yoga, the path of selfless work where work is done without desiring reward for it. Instead, all work is directed toward God-realization or self-realization or both.

Bhakti-yoga, the path of devotion to God, where all emotions are sublimated by turning them toward God, the way of experiencing God.

Jnana-yoga, the way of self-knowledge, Here knowledge is viewed as the primary path to moksa (liberation) and ignorance is seen as the root of all the ills of the world. It should be noted that jnana (knowledge) is not merely intellectual understanding but more often is understood to be experiential, intuitive knowledge gained from the *experience* of meditation, yoga, and other devotional practices.

As well as the different paths to realization identified in yoga, there are different *techniques* which often have, confusingly but not surprisingly, the same names. Some of the better known names and techniques are raja-yoga, bhakti-yoga, and jnana-yoga. While we identified the best known kinds of yoga in the preceeding pages, below we give a brief description of the kinds of disciplines used in each.

Just as many philosophical interpretations of yoga evolved, so too did many mind and body techniques evolve as disciplines to achieve the goals of each kind of yoga. All "schools" of yoga use concentration as their chief method but differ in defining the goal of concentration. Raja-yoga (the "kingly-yoga"), for example, uses concentration to lead to knowledge of the self, while bhakti-yoga, the path of religious devotion, uses concentration as the way to God-realization and jnana-yoga, the path of philosophical discrimination, uses concentration as the way to identify the individual self with the universal self. Amazingly, the disciplines of concentration that are still followed today around the world were outlined by Patanjali, a distinguished philosopher of the third century B.C., who emphasized the direct experience of reality.

Just as Western science concentrates and focuses attention on the outer, physical world, observing it, systematizing its facts and then drawing conclusions about its reality, so does Hindu yoga use concentration and focus of attention to explore the subjective world within, to make and test observations about it, to systematize its facts and draw conclusions about the nature of the inner world and about the mind and consciousness and the inner reality. Hindu philosophy has long defined the many different mind states that perceive reality differently, mind states the West is only slowly and begrudgingly acknowledging to exist. The specifics of the various yogic mental disciplines are too long to be included in this discussion, but many are now being found in Western literature.

The bewildering maze of Hindu philosophy is complicated by a second, also prehistorically derived tradition of a prescribed social order within human communities, the order we know as caste. Although historians conventionally discuss the three major castes of India, there are, in fact, scores of other caste distinctions within each major caste. Some of these are of long tradition, but new castes have come from the new economic levels modernization has thrust on Indian society. Whatever their origin, their effects are inextricably tied in with the Hindu philosophy of life.

Castes actually arose out of the four ancient classes of people in Indian society: the Brahmins (priests), the Kshatriyas (warriors), the Vaishyas (merchants), and the Sudras (the cultivators). All others were outcasts, and thus all the rejected eventually formed a fifth class, the Harijans (the untouchables).

Most Westerners, especially Americans, are shocked to learn that the caste system still exists in India. They have some vague familiarity with the three major castes and rock in their boots when they discover that, as one modern authority reports, "Hindu society is divided into a great number of castes, which amount to *some three thousand* today. The process of forming and absorbing castes still goes on."

I personally believe that not only was the caste system a remarkably practical solution to the rigors of early Indian development and a prime factor in creating the passivism of India, but caste distinctions made it possible for everyone to attain some satisfactions in life no matter how extreme the poverty of their circumstances might be. There is, no doubt, a fine line between the psychological satisfactions in life and spiritual satisfactions.

P.T. Raju, in his essay, "Religion and Spiritual Values in Indian Thought" (in *The Indian Mind,* edited by Charles A. Moore, East-West Center Press, University of Hawaii, 1967) tackles the question of whether Indian religion can lead to the realization of spiritual values (presumably as defined by Western philosophers). The essay is actually an attempt to clarify differences and similarities between "religion" and "spiritual philosophy" and as such provides interesting insights into how an erudite Indian views Western notions of religion and the pursuit of spiritual fulfillment. The reader may find these provocative topics for reflection.

Professor Raju sets down seven characteristics that qualify Indian philosophy and distinguish it from religion as the West understands religion. These are:

1. "Indian religion does not mean a fixed set of dogmas, doctrines, creeds, and rituals." There are many forms of Indian philosophy that relect the Hindu view and meaning of life.

2. "The word 'religion' is an English word meaning the tie to man's source of his being, particularly his material origins. In contrast, 'yoga' means the tie of man to the divine spirit.

3. "Indian religions have retained some of the most primitive forms of worship, giving them a symbolic value, and yet have developed the highest forms of religious thought and spiritual philosophy.

4. "According to Indian tradition, it is not necessary for a philosophy to accept the reality of God in order to be called spiritual. . . . What is their common characteristic (of the Indian philosophies) that entitles them to be called religious? The answer is: The conviction about the inwardness of man's conscious being.

5. "None of the Indian religions is a revealed religion. A revealed religion is one for which the divine truth is

revealed to a single founder. . . . Indian religions are reflective. (Their founders 'do not claim that the truth was revealed to them alone; everyone who cares to go through the necessary discipline and reflects on his experiences can reach the truth.')

6. "None of the Indian religions is a tribal religion. Yahveh is said to have been originally a local divinity, worshipped by a tribe; he later became the God of Israel, and still later the universal God. It is characteristic of tribal religions to insist upon a particular social and ethical code, which was originally the code of the tribe. A reflective religion does not insist upon a single code, but allows every group to follow its own code.

7. "It is said that some religions are universal, and others are particularist. Christianity and Islam are called universal, because they accept converts; Judaism and Hinduism are called particularist, because they do not accept converts." Dr. Raju then argues, quite logically, "If inward spirituality is the essential meaning of religion, then every religion in which every man can realize God thorough his own inwardness should be called universal and every religion which holds that such realization is possible only through faith in its own founder should be called particularist."

The Great Books of Hinduism
(all created before 100 A.D).

Bhagavad-Gita, a religious text and religious poem; part of the Mahabharata.
Mahabharata, a Sanscrit religious epic poem.

Ramayana, a Sanscrit epic about Rama, an important Hindu deity.
Rig-Veda, the original, ancient sacred Hindu hymns.
The Vedas, the four vedas that are the principal sacred scriptures of Hinduism.
Upanishads, the earliest philosophic discussions of the Vedas.

MAJOR AND
MINOR MIRACLES

As Westerners gain in affluence, they covet miracles less and less. Of course some still go to Lourdes or Fatima or make the long pilgrimage to Sai Baba in India, but nowadays few people harbor dreams of the miraculous. Visions of finding lost loves have become hazy. The West has had too many dreams come true: an abundance of food, cars, homes, planes, telephones, television, money in the pocket, and even welfare. Somatic man is satiated and for the most part his psychic longings are fantasies, submerged, barely conscious dreams to reveal the power of the spirit, not to move mountains. The Church, an earthly custodian of the psyche, has mandated miracles to be so rare as to be but one a century. In its turn science admonishes about the inexorable orderliness of nature and the limitations of human substance. Rational man has confirmed the probabilities of unusual events unexpectedly solving unsolvable problems to be so small that we can expect no surcease from the inevitable coursing of nature. Miracles cannot be expected nor hoped for.

It is not so in India. Miracles happen every day.

Two freshly hewn miracles were unfolded to me by the two beneficiaries of the psychic events. It began this way:

Just before one of my annual excursions to India, my Bombay friend Shireen decided to take a major step in her search for enlightenment. For a score or more years she has followed the mystic's quest with the same kind of confusion that every other thoughtful person has faced. Living in India does not guarantee easy access to the Right Path; on the contrary, the plethora of religious claimants to the Way of Truth serves only to increase one's uncertainty about the choice one should make. In older days most of us were molded spiritually by the small communities of our families, church ties and friends, and so it once was in India. But rapidly expanding communications and increased ease of travel have touched us all with the excitement of mysteries beyond the warming hearths of home, and they pose more questions than our minds can answer. Unless we have the rare fortune of finding a true guru or are blessed by revelations, no single philosophy of life seems to answer all our questions. The press of endless worldly unknowns on mind and spirit creates doubt, less about the reality of God or oneness, for inherently we lean on these hopes, but rather, our doubts are how to get in touch with God, or with the Universal Spirit.

And so it was with Shireen. A Zoroastrian (a Parsee), her well-born social position had, in recent years, exposed her more and more to the uncertainties of how to know the spiritual life. When I first met Shireen many years earlier through a patron of oriental arts, I would have not believed she would become such a serious resource for yogic philosophies and practices. A tiny, self-assured, well-connected lady, she took care of all her husband's business accounts and taxes and lived an active social life amongst diplomats and ambassadors in a special environment of devout and highly regarded Parsees. Parsees are the descendants of the Zoroastrian religion of ancient Persia that migrated to India in about the 10th century. Zoroastrianism is a unique synthesis of surprisingly modern concepts about life. It teaches that one's ultimate fate is self-determined by a free will and its philosophy can be summed up by its oft-repeated motto, "good thoughts, good words, good deeds," a charge for social activism, quite different from the Hindu injunctions for interiorization. Still, Zoroastrians feel the call of the mystical, and they explore, with great seriousness, all ways to fulfill the ultimate bliss and the final resurrection of all men without sin and without change.

It was almost with an air of resignation that Shireen decided upon her next step. Friends were making a pilgrimage to Monghyr (mon-geer) for the Swami Satyananda Golden Jubilee Convention. One could spend a few days listening to the Swami, take part in elementary classes in meditation (advanced classes are for initiates), and then, at week's end, receive darshan (blessing; also spiritual merit from a fulfilled presence) from the Swami. And if one were spiritually ready, one might receive a mantra. The mantra, syllables of primordial soundness, is the diving platform, the earthly reference of spiritual forces, whose repetition with single-mindedness bids consciousness to fill the mind and soar toward the vault of heaven.

It is not easy to travel to Monghyr. The closest a train comes is a day's bus trip away, and when spiritual congresses are held in India, there are never enough buses. Community dormitories are jammed, the kitchens run short of food, so if you are not an accomplished ascetic, it is best to go with blankets and food. The arrangements are typically Indian. The Indian mind is little concerned by groups, it is concerned only with the spiritual self and one mind.

Shireen's sojourn to Monghyr was more difficult than anticipated. Transportation strikes have long been a way of life in India, and the small group of pilgrims from Bombay was forced to hire a succession of cars and bullock carts. It took twenty hours of travel from the train stop to reach the encampment, and to the high-caste pilgrims, it was a disappointing sight. The ashram buildings were small and unimpressive, mixtures of stone and baked adobe, stained by the elements and looking forlorn on the expanses of the salt-and-pepper sandy soil. Pilgrims began to fill the fields with moving forms, the women painting the fields with color as they strolled in bright saris, smoke from their cooking pots sketching in the lines. It was quiet but expectant. There is a quietness in spiritual meetings in India like no place else on earth. There is, too, an eagerness even in the quiet, an eagerness of mind and spirit. Any sense of people is lost in the turning of each person into himself, uniting with the guru and with the consciousness beyond. Here in the Monghyr fields, stretched long and wide with crowding bodies, the Swami's gentle voice could be heard at any distance. But it was hot, so hot that squatting at attention for hours led to quiet fainting. Nor was this discomfort all; contamination of food and water exhausted the toilet facilities of the nearby fields.

It is not easy being a pilgrim in India, yet Shireen endured it with spiritual devotion. She carried out every instruction. She rose early and did yogic exercises (the postures), she fasted, and she meditated. In the beginning she was troubled, for as she tried to meditate, she felt more keenly than ever the lack of an interior guide. She had no mantra, no holy sounds to vibrate within and tune the mind, no guru's gem that could lead the mind to consciousness of the cosmos. For Shireen was still searching. She had no guru and no mantra.

She was, of course, aware that the power of the mantra comes from the sacred use of sacred words. And she was not so naive as to believe she could not chance upon a proper mantra, particularly here in Monghyr where she so urgently felt the need for holy syllables. Descended through centuries from unbroken generations of Parsees, she was well equipped in the sacred theology of Zoroastrianism, and so, with a spiritual determination and a devotion to Zoroastrian scripture, she chose some ancient syllables from ancient Persian prayers to Zoroaster, and gave herself an unusual non-Hindu mantra.

It seemed ideal, a mantra she was comfortable with, one that sustained her over the long hours of meditation. At times its mere repetition seemed to lift her being to another plane where the nagging minutiae of life's experiences no longer came to mind, where at times mind seemed to be touched with glimpses of knowing all and the nothingness of

all. After meditation, listening to Swamiji, she would sometimes wonder whether perhaps the guru's mantra might be
even more powerful and guide her toward Eternal Bliss.

At week's end came darshan. Shireen was determined
to ask Swamiji for a mantra, but the day of darshan started with
long lines seeking his blessing long before dawn. Some fifty
thousand devotees would wait this day in silence, patient for
the smallest sound of spiritual blessing. Shireen joined the
line. By noon her feet were numb. It was unbearably hot.
Friends brought her food and water. It was past five o'clock
when she reached the Swami's chair.

He gave her darshan and then, before she could speak,
he said, "You've come to ask me for a mantra, but there is no
need. You already have a mantra. It is . . . ," naming the sacred
Zoroastrian syllables that only Shireen knew.

That should be story enough, but in India, as I said,
miracles are everyday.

It happened that Shireen described this recent experience one afternoon when we were gathered on the long, open
marble balcony at Shireen's, talking with Fali, a vigorous
young businessman whose unusual experiences with meditation I was documenting. It was the first time she had revealed
the incident. Fali sat stunned for a moment. Swami Satyananda
was Fali's guru; Fali too had gone to Monghyr for the convention but with a different group, and Fali too was Zoroastrian.

"Oh Shireen," he cried, "my guru has such great powers. I shall tell you only one thing he told me at my initiation.
Almost the same thing happened to me. Because of my wife's
devotion to Swamiji, long before I ever went to hear him talk,
I began to follow his instructions as he had taught my wife. I,

too, had no mantra, but I could think of nothing more meaningful and holy than certain words of our own Zoroastrian
prayers. So I chose my own mantra from those words. It was
not until six months later that Swamiji came to Bombay. At
darshan I asked him if he could give me a mantra for meditation. And just as for you, he said, "But you already have a
mantra," and he told me exactly the words I had chosen from
the old Pahlavi texts. Now I ask you, who is not a Parsee
would know our sacred texts?"

Shireen and Fali sat quiet, musing, I guessed, on the
spiritual powers of the swami. But my mind was churning
furiously. I was comparing East and West, struck by the differences in attitudes about these extraordinary experiences. Here
in Bombay my friends were in an enraptured transport of the
spirit. At home, in the West, there would be a fascination with
psychic phenomena and feverish speculation on the magic
rather than on the message. But here in India there are no
questions about the powers of spirit. They are not magical,
they are the reality.

For some time my friends remained absorbed in their
communion with the joys of spirit while my analytic, scientific
mind searched for keys to explain the ease with which they
slipped into self-communion and why we Westerners are so
much more inclined to resist succumbing to the ethereal embraces of the universal spirit. Then as my mind began to tease
apart the many different influences between East and West
behavior, still another thought intruded. How curious, I
thought, while they are lost in spiritual meditation, my mind
is focusing on trying to understand a here-and-now experience
of spiritual behavior, and in a way that, too, is a spiritual

meditation. For, if I discipline my mind with single purpose to understand the way of their enlightenment, I may chance upon insights I might never otherwise know. They are, I admitted to myself, on a very different plane, with values and aspirations and a discipline of mind that we Westerners are only now beginning to recognize but still do not understand.

I thought about Western attitudes, about how we prefer to be spiritually led instead of forging individual paths, how we prefer being spiritual in congregations rather than alone, and how much we fear losing the individual, conspicuous nature of our minds to some unknown, uncontrollable, alien and mysterious agency such as a universal consciousness.

Seekers of spiritual knowledge in the West rely much more on the consensus of spiritual communities. There seems to be a need to validate one's personal spiritual feelings by an outward display, some need to prove to others one's spiritual nature. For the most part Westerners prefer being spiritual as members of a group.

In India no one really cares who is what religion nor how one outwardly demonstrates spiritual feelings. Spirituality is very much one's own business; congregations of worshippers exist because holy places and holy people offer ways to spiritual progress. In India spiritual devotees are individuals who are grouped by circumstance. They do not belong to any group in the sense of community, rather they choose this or that holy place or guru because of deeply personal, not collective nor mutual, need or desire. It is the personal solitariness of spiritual voyages that distinguishes the Indian from the Western religious.

These differences only scratched the surface, I knew, and they are all related because they are all shaped by the same fundamental differences in beliefs. Take the swami's perfectly accurate report of not just one, but both of my friends' most private, unspoken thoughts. The Western mind, so firmly guided by the orderly, inflexible rules of science, seizes upon the phenomenon, first to classify it (as mind-reading) and then to search for explanations of the hows and whys of the phenomenon. We of the West seem to have a compulsion to analyze . . . to know . . . not by the impress of experience, but in terms of operational principles; and the reason for this compulsion is because we depend so heavily on *proving* the reality of one thing or another. The interesting thing about proofs and proving is that they are carried out largely to convince *other people.* The need for consensus by reliable proof is vital for the material life, the West believes, because it enables control over physical nature, and the scientific ways of proving phenomena are infinitely more efficient than consensus by impressions. But our fascination with the power of science makes us forget that the practical reality of science is a special reality of what science has set down as the rules of nature and this special reality of the *material* universe may or may not be found to hold true for events of mind and spirit.

The Indian, on the other hand, makes a sharp distinction between the practical reality of nature and science and the spiritual reality. The psychic powers of the swami are the natural flow of spiritual energies from enlightened states, from a unity of self with endless resources of the universal spirit. The Indian has no need to intellectualize spiritual messages, the Indian *experiences* community of spirit. The difference

between analyzing phenomena and absorbing their meaning
by opening the mind to receive them through direct experience is a difference in the way cultures perceive the organization of the universe. Indian culture began by seeing man as
part of the cosmic forces.

When human beings first began to formalize their relationships with the vast forces of the universe, it was as if the
world became split in two. Toward the West man assigned the
highest powers to beings so supreme the supernal vision could
be fulfilled only in heaven, and then only after recognizing
sovereignty of a supreme being. Toward the East man somehow came to feel his very being expressed kinship with the
flow of nature, and that union with the universal energy could
be achieved using the mind's awareness to identify more
closely with the essence of the universal force. The East discovered early that it is the experience that enlightens.

I began to wonder whether the yoga and TM (transcendental meditation) and spiritual communities the reckless van-
guard of psychotherapy experienced in the 70s is the foundation of our new open, sharing, self-examining, experiential
psychotherapy that is so widely practiced today.

There is, too, a deeper, more psyche-absorbing change
that has been shaping Western appreciations of the inner
being. As the West has come more and more to explore the
philosophies of India, more and more we have heard the word
"ineffable." There were no English words to express the sense
or unsense of states of supra-consciousness. The best we could
do was to use "ineffable" to express the kind of knowing that
lies beyond words. My own examination of the quintessential
consciousness (*Supermind,* 1980) suggests our lack of words to

describe experiences of the spirit and psyche, such as samadhi, is because experiences of higher states of consciousness have no physical equivalents and so cannot form images for recall. The West's growing acceptance of subjective experience as real and valid comes closer and closer to the way the sages of India perceived mind and consciousness so many centuries ago. Many experienced philosophers and therapists of the West are working to achieve integration of the perceptions of self and the meaning of life of both East and West to have, as Huxley wrote, "the best of both worlds."

THE TIBETAN
LIGHT BALLS

It started as an ordinary excursion up from Bombay to Juhu Beach to have tea with Jinni, not that any meeting with Jinni could ever be ordinary. It was the same Jinni who, as an American college girl, came to India, married an Indian and did not return to the States for twenty-five years, the same Jinni who was the first devotee of the later world famous Swami Mukdananda (her Baba), the Jinni who discovered the extraordinary seventeenth century collection of palace furnishings and used them to decorate one of the Maharana's palaces when it became a famous hotel, the same Jinni who endured twenty-five years as the wife of an alcoholic, spoiled and violent Indian, bore him three children then adopted an itinerant Tibetan's son, and the same Jinni who has lived now in self-imposed exile for five years. Incredibly, when Jinni was commissioned to write Baba's biography and when she insisted on writing the whole truth, she was expelled from the ashram.

Jinni was in especially high spirits when we arrived at her small cottage. Always cheery and remarkably extrovert despite a consuming devotion to the spiritual life, Jinni's communication and body movement were like sparklers on the Fourth of July. She was motherly large and motherly energetic, always looking splendidly warm and loving in her Indian saris, the kind of ideal woman-friend-mother you always wanted to touch and talk and be with. From the twinkling eyes to the brief warm touches, Jinni always showered you with the joy of being joyful. If Jinni had a single fault, it was her elusiveness. It was next to impossible to pin her down to a date. If the time and place of a meeting suited her vague, never-explained schedule or her mood or the needs of her pocketbook, then we could have the pleasure of her company. Much of the time she simply disappeared into the back country, surfacing only to earn a bit of money. Her skill as an interior decorator made her much sought after in Bombay, and once commissioned, she never shirked the job or failed to keep a date. Otherwise she floated in her freedom, unaware of any pull to simple social communion. After years of waiting for my rare dialogues with Jinni, I finally came to realize that her whole inner being was in some way always with a consciousness beyond the sphere of mind the rest of us know and it allowed her earthly self to visit us only occasionally.

On this occasion Jinni was in a state of quiet ecstasy. No sooner than we were settled with our tea when Jinni ran to her bedroom and returned with a tiny bottle she placed on the table before me.

"I saved these for you," she said. I picked up the tiny glass bottle (a miniature perfume bottle) and saw it contained a half dozen or more small brown seeds. Before I could ask, Jinni began her story.

Some two weeks before my arrival, Jinni had been visited by a small band of Tibetan lamas travelling on pilgrimage to Buddhist holy places. I doubt if there is any religious faithful anywhere in India or Nepal or Tibet who has not heard of Jinni, and I'm sure many a Tibetan knows that she became the guardian of a Tibetan boy. In any event, the lamas sought out Jinni much as any pilgrim seeks out a colleague in the holy quest for enlightenment.

Once every few years, as lamas gather to start a pilgrimage, they conduct a ritual that is to protect them as they travel and, since the pilgrimage itself gives spiritual merit, the protection extends to the whole life of the pilgrim. The ritual consists of the group of lamas chanting over a fragment of a relic of a Buddhist saint. Usually it is one or two hairs from the head. As the chanting accelerates and becomes more intense, the tiny relic becomes fiery red with heat, turns white-hot and begins to grow in size. The ritual then changes. The chanting slows, the relic begins to cool and finally breaks into dozens of tiny brown balls that look like little seeds.

"They are the dzu," Jinni told me. "Dzu means holy light balls because they come from the white heat of the relic. They have the power to protect the blessed from all the major difficulties of life except death. Moreover, every time you escape a disaster and are protected, the number of light balls will increase."

Jinni reached for another bottle on the table. "See these," she said, "only last week there were just a dozen. Then I had a near tragedy at the courts (India is loath to grant divorces), but at the last minute I won an important point and my case was continued. Now look. There are eighteen light balls in the bottle, and it has been sealed all the time."

I looked in my bottle.

"I had to divide up what the lamas gave me. They told me to give some to you when I told them you were coming," Jinni began to explain. "Anyway, there are seven light balls in your bottle. And notice that I sealed it twice to make sure you wouldn't lose any. Remember to count them if you should have any serious problems. You'll know how fortunate you have been to escape something serious happening to you, and you'll find that the light balls have multiplied." We all then dutifully counted the tiny balls, over and over. There were, absolutely, seven light balls.

It was always exciting to be with Jinni. I was especially pleased to be considered a close enough friend to be given the precious light balls. It touches me deeply whenever the spirit of India includes me as belonging to it.

I didn't know then how soon my light balls would be tested. My Bombay travelling companion, Shireen, and I were leaving the following day on one of our excursions around India, this time to the southwest areas, to Cochin, Trivandrum and on to Kovalum Beach.

Cochin is a strange and wonderful place. It is a giant network of inland waterways, great canals and lagoons lined with Chinese style dipping (fishing) nets and stray freighters working their ways toward tiny industrial plants hidden in the jungle overgrowth. It is the remnant site where the Jews emigrated before the fourth century, and where the marvelous synagogue with its exquisite floor of hundreds of blue porcelain tiles, each with a different scene, was built in 1568 and still survives. Closer to the heart of Cochin, the Syrian-Christian church shows its monuments.

Cochin, in the state of Kerala, is also home to the Kathakali dancers. Shireen and I spent several days absorbing the sights and sounds of Cochin topping off one very busy day by an evening of watching the incredible Kathakali dancers. Always boys and men, the dancers are trained for years in the special art of communicating the messages of the dance through their eyes. The hands and feet are used only to extend the symbolism of their bright green make-up.

The next morning I was eager to walk about the marvelous tropical surroundings of the hotel and lagoons. I slipped out of my bed quietly so not to waken Shireen and reached for the antique ring I always put on the nightstand while I sleep. I slipped it on my finger and shuddered with a strange feeling. Looking down, I saw to my horror that its priceless cameo was missing altogether. The ring—nearly 400 years old—had been handed down in my family for generations. But its true value was that it was virtually all I had in remembrance of my entire family, now all gone.

Even at six in the morning everyone in the hotel was eager to help look for the cameo. The sweepers and groundskeepers and bearers searched the hotel from top to bottom, turning over every wisp of dust and peeking in every corner. There is no one more sympathetic and helpful than an Indian helping you in times of trouble. Even the crew of a French ship laying in for repairs all pitched in to look. They called the boat company and the boat we had been in was searched, and they found and searched the taxi, too. All I could think of was how very dust-dirt color this unique cameo was and that no one could distinguish it from the earth or dust.

Shireen came down and upon hearing the news, joined in with new ideas and more searching went on. Finally we all gave up. I insisted it was now a closed chapter. It had been a good search, but looking for a small stone the color of the world was, indeed, hopeless. Shireen and I went into the restaurant for breakfast. My cheeks were still stained from tears that carried so many memories of family and its one heirloom that everyone had cherished. I was choked with sadness.

Suddenly there was a shout, and despite custom and the rules of caste behavior and hotel decorum, in burst a sweeper, a slight figure in his work khaki and bare feet. He shouted and held up his fist, clutching the ring. "Found it, found it!" he cried. And the whole hotel rejoiced. He had gone to our room and scoured it, finally spying the dust-colored cameo behind a loose baseboard.

Breakfast suddenly became wonderful. At leisure and at peace, Shireen and I went up to our sun filled open room. Then I remembered.

"The light balls," I cried. "Let's look at the light balls to see if they have multiplied—certainly for me nearly losing my precious ring was a major distaster that was averted."

We counted the light balls. Six? Only six? Shireen counted. Yes, only six. We sat stunned. Two days ago there were seven and the bottle was still firmly sealed. Now there were only six light balls. Truly I had used the energy of an entire light ball to save my precious ring.

Back in Bombay Jinni was unbelieving. Her light balls had never multiplied again, but on the other hand, she hadn't lost any, either. She was puzzled and said she would ask the lamas when she saw them again. But I don't think she ever did.

Years later, in Bangkok I asked John Blofeld about the light balls. After all, he had lived and studied with Tibetan Buddhists and had reached the highest levels of the mystical, magical Tantric Buddhism of Tibet. "Yes," he said, those are the dzu, the light balls that protect against life's disasters. But I can't tell you more." And he didn't.

The Kite and the Crows

The ring had been recovered. I was relaxing in the luxury of our marvelously old-world, tropically styled hotel room. Long, wide, and sunny but still cool, I could watch through the great windows as bits of backwater Cochin life passed by. Not twenty yards ahead was a small, clear channel for the smaller trades boats, the oarsmen poling or hoisting a bit of sail according to their mood. I could see baskets of tropical fruits, coconuts, fresh fish and masses of flowers all on their way to market. Beyond I could watch as the boats hugged the shoreline when they drifted out of the channels into the busy headwaters of the bay. As I watched the lazy scene unfold, a large white bird flew into the tree outside my window that I immediately recognized as a kite. There was a flurry on the branch and I saw that several crows perched there were fluttering their wings to keep their balance after the impact of the kite's landing.

Since I adore all animals and birds and know something about their habitats, I was surprised that a kite was in this lowland countryside. I had seen kites before in the California hills and recognized the great white bird with black bars on its wings. Kites also make a funny screeching call, much like hawks protecting their nests. I knew, too, that kites were solitary birds and although they could be found in hawk country, they maintain a separate territory. Kites and hawks constantly guard their homelands by using long sweeping forays around the borders, screeching all the while.

Yet here was a kite on the inland waterway, in as tropical a setting as one could find. He was perched, awkwardly, on a slender branch of a Royal Poinciana tree, so large a bird that the branch kept swaying and he would have to tilt and spread his wings with every twist of his head. He was, perhaps, twice the size of the crows he had disturbed. Crows, of course, swarm over India, curious half-raven birds with broad lavender-grey neck bands and enormous beaks.

The kite moved to a sturdier branch nearby and a surprising thing happened. First one crow, then a second and a third followed the kite from branch to branch, sometimes to the ground and back to a branch again. One crow in particular was always close to the kite, swooping in to land on the same branch, unbalancing the kite who would then flutter desperately to stay in balance. If the kite flew to the ground to feed, the three crows came too, and they would peck at the kite. Sometimes when the kite flew to a high branch, two of the crows would fly there and hover over him and the kite would turn and lunge at them with his curved beak.

I was completely puzzled by the continuing drama. Finally I saw the kite land in a nearby tree. One crow, more slender than the others, flew in and landed on a branch just below the kite. Then I saw the kite reach down with his beak, the young crow opened wide his beak just as young crows do with their parents when they are fed. The kite popped an insect into the crow's open beak. Immediately the other two young crows flew in and began to fuss and the activity began all over again. The kite was feeding the crows! Was the kite an adoptive parent to the young crows? What else could explain his behavior? He tolerated the incessant cawing of the crows and their pestering and he fed them. Once more I had been privileged to witness the miraculous.

THE SHADOW
ASTROLOGER

The three of us, Jinni, Shireen, and I had been on a picnic excursion to the Kanheri caves some 30 miles north of Bombay. Actually I thought we were going to visit the Canary caves until someone spelled it out for me (I hadn't done my tourist homework). Despite any auditory confusion, the Kanheri caves are truly an awesome sight no matter how lowly they may rate as a tourist attraction. It was the first time I had seen places where communities of Buddhist religious had lived at the time the Christian era began.

The caves are variously dated between 200 B.C. and 200 A.D. and there is not much left of the religious carvings and statues that no doubt furnished the halls for worship. There is, in fact, so little interest in the Kanheri caves (even though it is a National Park) that one popular guide book claims not a single statue of Buddha remains. There are, nonetheless, two statues of Buddha, both in one small room and in a most unusual arrangement—they face each other. But the Buddhas are on the second level of caves where neither tourists nor tourist guide book writers seem to venture.

I began to daydream about being a Buddhist monk two thousand years ago, living in the crude, tiny cubicles where contemplative monks once lived and that spoke of sacrifice and renunciation of the material luxuries of the world. Suddenly I became aware of a startling contradiction in the incredible scene around me. The smallish hills made for smallish self-contained valleys, protected from the nearby sea, and these valley were bursting with every glory nature could provide. Trees heavy with bananas, figs, and oranges hid giant pineapple plants. There were patches of enormous cauliflower and cabbages, and everywhere you looked there was an endless cornucopia of fruits and vegetables and nuts and all of it surrounded by the oranges and reds of hibiscus, azalea, and trailing morning glory vines. (The importance of the region's generous fertility to contemplative life is also described in the story of the holy man, a contemplative who lived in a nearby valley, p. 93.) Stunned by the contrast between the harshness of the caves inside and the epicurean delights outside, I noted aloud that the monks may have lived in dusty sparseness inside but they certainly had Paradise outside.

My Indian friend Shireen is always quick to catch my strange observations. This time she was also piqued to think that these long ago religious, revered throughout history as the ultimate ascetics could be thought to, perhaps, live indulgently. They had been, after all, acclaimed through history as monks who had denied themselves every pleasure to spend their lives in meditation and they were the heroes of one of the world's greatest religions. I didn't dare tell Shireen that I was also wondering if this is where the notion of the pot-bellied Buddha came from. Certainly life here must have been just as divine gastronomically and esthetically as it was contemplatively.

It did rather make me wonder whether our ideas of asceticism and "dying to the flesh" and self-denial might be more myth than truth. My daydreaming transported me to "visions of sugarplums" and my mouth watered in epicurean delight as I swung my eyes through a 180 degree arc of the most elegant food nature could provide. And of course my sardonic self wondered, too, whether the Buddhist Gardens of Eden in India had had their transgressors the way Adam and Eve had betrayed the trust that gave them Eden. The thought brought up all kinds of interesting speculations about history and religion and myths and reality. As my friend Shireen said, "You are the only person I know who would think of things like that." And I hadn't even told her about the fat Buddha.

I had filled the bare caves with images that may have been more real than historical. And, I was thinking, if meditation and contemplation could lead to joyful bliss, then perhaps the contemplative life of the early Buddhist monks was much more joyful than ascetic and bare and filled with rigor and hardship.

Just then I heard Jinni shout, and looking down to the path by the first level of caves, I saw a tall, husky, fair-skinned saddhu striding up the path.

"Swamiji," Jinni shouted, then she turned to us.

"That's Swami Arananda," she explained. "He's an American—has an ashram in California." I groaned to myself. California, of course. *I should have known* was all I could think.

Descending to join him we learned he was "bumming" his way back to Bombay after having been on a pilgrimage to a small religious community nearby. Of course, we all chorused, we'd love to give him a ride.

And he was a jolly fellow who merged smoothly into my daydreams of the fat and happy monks who had lived in this Paradise. Anyone else would have been out of place in my dream.

At Juhu we stopped to leave Jinni, but of course we all had to stay for tea. Somehow we were keyed up, rather much as if we had all sipped of the same spiritual ambrosia. Swami Arananda said one of the things he wanted to do in Bombay was to see the shadow astrologer.

Our spirits, already soaring, leaped into mega-flight. New adventures and new secrets of the future buzzed around our heads in excited confusion. We learned that the shadow astrologer was very famous, that he advised heads of states and princesses and movie stars and the very, very rich. We almost mobbed Swami Arananda to see if we, too, could see the shadow astrologer before we left Bombay the following day.

Jinni made some quick phone calls, then frantically told us that if we could hurry into Bombay before the sun was too far down, the shadow astrologer would see us. We darned near broke our necks getting out the door. Even Shireen's driver became caught up in the excitement and he hurried us through the most vicious of Bombay's traffic, delivering us at the astrologer's residence around five o'clock when the shadows were thickening fast.

Like most people in Bombay, the shadow astrologer lived in a tall apartment house building. We fussed over the slowness of the elevator but finally arrived at his door. After the briefest of introductions by Shireen, when we learned the astrologer did not speak English, he hurried us back to the elevator explaining we were going up to the roof. On the roof he positioned us with our backs to the sinking sun, got out a pretty, clear plastic ruler and began to measure. He measured a dozen distances across the hands and some shadows of our arms then said that, quite frankly, he would have to guess about the total height of our shadows that had already stretched over and beyond the parapet wall.

Measurements done, we returned to his apartment. There we sat by the astrologer's desk and he pulled out a modestly sized book looking to be of fine, soft parchment and perhaps a hundred or more pages. Shireen translated the explanation that this was a compendium summarizing the lives of previous incarnations. I assumed the previous lives were catalogued according to dates and certain shadow statistics, but that was all the information I could get. Then the reading started.

Shireen translated the shadow astrologer's words. I had, he was saying, just finished writing a book about the mind and body (true) and that it would become widely read (later proved to be true), and that I would become well known and write many other books. He then went on to say that I would write several books on human consciousness and unusual mind states. I protested. I have no thought of doing anything like that, I said. But he became quite agitated and Shireen could scarcely keep up her translation. He insisted I would write about consciousness and would also write a book about India. He's crazy, I thought. But that was before I wrote all those books he said I would write.

The episode is strongly linked in my mind with an another episode on a day in Jaipur. It was a different trip to India, this time touring with friends. Rick, a successful and very serious physician, was a complete skeptic about anything magical or mysterious or supernatural. All baloney, he said.

One afternoon Rick set out to walk around the enormous grounds of the Rambagh Palace Hotel that had once been the Maharaja's palace while his wife Katy and I decided to go for a swim in the great dank mausoleum that contained the Maharaja's old swimming pool. An hour later, as we walked back to the hotel, Rick saw us and came running. He was very excited.

"You're never going to believe this," he exhaled in a near frenzy. "I've just met the most incredible man. I was just walking along, strolling, sort of, and this old chap stopped me and said, 'Rick, would you like to talk to me?' I figured he was just an old beggar trying to hit me for money, so I said no. Then he said, 'You were one of five children. Your oldest sister's name is Elizabeth.' That really shook me up because no one in India could possibly know those things. So I sat down with him and you can't believe what he told me."

All in all, Rick told us, as he kept repeating how no one would ever believe him, the old Indian had played back his life like a phonograph record. "I don't see how anyone could know all those things," he kept saying, "I wonder how he did it. I've got to find out how he does that trick."

"A trick," Rick kept repeating.

"Fortune-telling" experiences like Rick's and like mine abound in India but never, never if you go looking for them. One peculiarity these kinds of psychic experiences in India share with those elsewhere in the world is that they never come from wishful thinking or any other kind of setting of the psychic stage. And unfortunately for true believers in psychic phenomena, such experiences seem to happen more often to skeptics than to believers.

When it was their turn a few years later, my UCLA tour group was predictably excited about the prospect of psychic readings. Nearly everyone wanted readings despite my warnings that a crowd would tax the shadow astrologer's energies unfairly. The group settled on five lucky participants by drawing lots and Shireen made the arrangements. I chose not to accompany the group, a decision, it turned out, to be most fortunate.

As I later interpreted Shireen's recounting, none of the readings went well. The shadow astrologer's descriptions about previous life events, the group all agreed, had absolutely no resemblance to fact for any of them. From the first reading on the group interrupted, argued, and voiced disapproval, making, I guessed, the shadow astrologer uncomfortable and interfering with his concentration. For whatever reason, the experience was a disaster. Since the shadow astrologer was so highly regarded around the world, I was puzzled by his apparent failure with the five of the tour group.

As a trained analyst of phenomena, to make sense out of the disaster I knew I had to balance any consensus about the astrologer's widely acclaimed successes against his failure with my group. The failure seemed to be an irrefutable fact; on the other hand, such a conclusion could just as well be suspect coming as it did from the confusion of translating Gujarati to English and the group's babble. Both could have distorted the information intended by the astrologer. It is often reported that all psychic phenomena are easily disrupted by confusion and negative emotions. Of course the worldwide acclaim of the astrologer's psychic powers might be more wishful thinking than reality.

Finally I faced my own experience of a few years earlier. It was solid, verified evidence that the shadow astrologer's predictions of the future could, indeed, be remarkably accurate. I decided to withhold conclusions about my tour group's luck or their relationship to the stars. Perhaps they simply were not travelling in the astral plane of India.

THE HOLY MAN

It was not too far from the Kanheri Caves, but because I vowed not to reveal his whereabouts, that is as close as I can come to describing the holy man's private retreat. Naturally it was Jinni who knew this rarest of spiritual saddhus and led us to him. I did not know what to expect in meeting a spiritual recluse, but most of us carry a vague image of hermit contemplatives as bent, elderly, white-bearded, emaciated semi-skeletons in faded saffron robes. It is as if we insist there must be some sign of awful suffering before we can be convinced about spiritual devotion, as if we are all masochists of the spirit. Even when Jinni said we would have to hike a few miles into the countryside, I was still gung ho to see a real, live contemplative. I never once thought about cobras in the brush or scorpions or fire ants under every leaf.

We did, in fact, walk nearly two miles through tropical overgrowth before Jinni rapturously announced we were there. We stood on a low bluff looking down upon a small lush valley no larger than the size of a football field. The floor of the valley was filled with cultivated fruit trees and giant vegetable plants, bordered all around by tall banana trees blending softly into the hills that bounded the tiny valley.

We threaded our way through the fruit trees and giant cabbages finally emerging into a small clearing. We stopped, hushed, and my heart stood still.

There, before us was the wide mouth of a cave, and just inside was the holy man, asleep.

Seventeen years earlier he had vowed never to speak and never to sit or lie down again in mortal life, acts he dedicated to God as evidence of his devotion to the universal spirit and his single-minded quest for union with God.

It was the tenderest of scenes. A tall, well-built man with black hair curling down upon his shoulders stood upright, except for his neck and head bent to rest on a padded swing suspended from the ceiling of the cave. Nearby a young, vigorous acolyte, smiling in great happiness, moved silently in preparation for the monk's awakening. About ten feet to the left of the sling was a small shrine carved from the side of the cave. It had small double-doors that the acolyte now opened to signal the presence of Kali's spirit and the moment of reverence. Jinni had told us that the holy man slept from noon until three, and that precisely at three the bell of the shrine would sound and the holy man would awaken to brief devotions to Kali. After that he would receive us.

The holy man stirred, lifted his head a bit, rubbed his eyes, looked at us standing mutely in front of him and broke into the most engaging laugh and smile of greeting I have ever experienced. In an instant he had transformed us all into bundles of delighted spirits, eager to absorb the ecstasy of spirit union this special man created. From uncertainty and awe, he had led us into the warmth of his spirit. As the monk silently recited a brief devotion, the acolyte spread a woven grass mat for us so we could sit facing the holy man. The acolyte then sat in a semi-yoga posture a few feet to the side and front of the holy man. Jinni, of course, knew what to do. She first asked about the holy man's health, then asked whether any devotees had visited.

The conversation flowed so naturally it was difficult to realize that while *we* were talking to the holy man, he was answering us without ever saying a word. Whenever we said anything, the acolyte would turn slightly to his guru, tilt his head as if listening, turn toward us, then, still smiling broadly, give us the holy man's answer. It was not until later that I realized the holy man had never uttered a word.

We were asked to stay for tea. Incongruous? Not at all. As we all relaxed and began to walk around, I could see the extraordinary haven the holy man and his acolyte had made. The half-dug-out cave offered protection from the monsoon rains, but did not block out the sunlight that poured down upon the valley floor. I saw every kind of tropical fruit tree imaginable, from avocado to mango, and toward one side was what I felt surely must be a miracle garden. Every plant, whether rows of carrots or giant pineapple, produced its fruits lavishly, yet not a single weed grew between the rows. Surely in the tropical mix of moisture and sunshine weeds must grow as well as fruits and vegetables, yet none could be seen. Did these two men work incessantly to cultivate their garden and groves? I thought not—there was no sign of weeding, no sign of cultivation. The food simply grew to their pleasure. I was in awe.

As the acolyte prepared our tea, the holy man walked about. In actual fact, he seemed to bound about, striding with great pleasure, smiling and laughing all the while, making us welcome and joyous with him. (In my pragmatic American way, I wondered whether laughing counted as speaking. In my rigid world of science any sound issuing from the vocal chords would be a violation of silence. But here, happiness of spirit was permitted, and anyway, the holy man's vow was not to speak. He hadn't made a vow about laughing.)

It was a great tea party. Tea was a blend of natural herbs and served in halves of coconut shells (rather well worn, I saw). Our plates were giant banana leaves and the acolyte came around with a selection of fruit. There was also a portion of absolutely incredible cake, baked from fruits of the garden and sweetened with sugar cane growing nearby. Neither the holy man nor his acolyte ate with us, the acolyte telling us they would eat later after devotions. Time for devotions was approaching and with great reluctance we said our good-byes.

There was much to think about as we walked the miles back to the road and our car. I was truly overwhelmed by the spirit that pervaded the tiny valley. It was very nearly the exact opposite of what my education and culture had led me to expect. Here was no austere contemplative, unapproachable and unresponsive, bound to endure eternal hardship. This was no scene of unending contemplation and prayer, no hair-shirting *mea culpa* punishment, no self-flagellation for the sins of the world. Here, secluded from human distraction, was the joy of knowing the spirit of the self and its union with all the universe. And it was a joy to be shared.

One sad observation intruded upon my reverie of affection. My eyes, trained to detect disharmonies, focused compellingly on the holy man's legs. Streaking across the soft brown skin of his beautifully formed and still strong legs were lines of dark, dusky blue-gray and stains of darkened red. I knew that gangrene was not far away. Years later I heard that he had stood until he could stand no longer. His acolyte took him to the hospital where, with smiling grace, he died with a smile so sweet it moved the entire hopital to a new devotion. I know I shall never forget the brief time I was with him.

SAI BABA:
PART I

In the late 60s and early 70s, the avant-counterculturists in the States were just beginning to discover the mental benefits of meditation and the philosophies of the Orient. When very popular and public figures like the Beatles revealed their meditative intercourse with the Maharishi, a number of tiny but long-established spiritual communities blossomed into public domain, communities such as the Vedantist groups endorsed by Huxley and Isherwood, Western devotees of Aurobindo or Satya Sai Baba and other gurus. As the spiritual frenzy over the philosophies of India spread, there were titillating reports about still another guru, this time a guru who was both spiritual leader and miracle man. In 1971 a book appeared to witness this new phenomenon: *Baba,* by Arnold Schulman (The Viking Press, 1971).

The rumors about Baba's powers were sensational. He could heal with a touch and cure with a blessing. One widely heralded miracle was the thrice raising from the dead of J.C. Collins (see p. 128). Baba's most tantalizing power, was, however, his reported ability to materialize precious physical elements. There were a hundred stories about the rubies and diamonds and gold jewelry he could pluck from thin air.

To me the story of Sai Baba illustrates the enduring paradox of how the Indian perceives reality. Whether Indians foster allegorical, metaphorical interpretations of life as practical, efficient ways to survive both the physical hardships and the primitive, unsophisticated mentality of an emergent humanity, I do not know. Certainly India developed in the confines of a most difficult physical environment and it has survived, also, the murderous assaults of invaders by its passive nonresistance. Indian history, for example, is a captivating mix of folklore and myth with bits of fact and no one, it seems, can be certain which is which.

I suspect that when the American sits back to think about India or about his Indian experience, if lived only vicariously in retreats with Swamis, there is often the strange feeling of wonder about why the beliefs and behavior of the people of India are so much like the beliefs and behavior of Indians more than 5000 years ago. Recent archeological finds, for example, have uncovered remnants of completely unfortified, passivist communities and there are scores of small carved figures of yogis sitting in the lotus position, meditating.

Life developed much differently in the Western hemisphere. We in the West change our beliefs and behaviors dramatically, decade after decade. Although today some do embrace the Fundamentalist's resolve with as much fervor as did the most outspoken Puritan, most Westerners today behave and believe according to myriads of new notions about the nature of human beings and their destiny. It is not so in India.

How well I remember Mohinder. He could have posed for one of those ancient religious figures. By one of the chance encounters that mark my time in India, I had been guided to Mohinder as a source of especially interesting information about Sai Baba.

My taxi man could not believe the address where I expected to find Mohinder. The address was in the outlying slums of Calcutta—not the worst, to be sure, but in a district where roads were neither bricked nor pounded and where street names and addresses were most often unknown. I had been given Mohinder's name by an Indian acquaintance who had met him at a local religious celebration. My Indian friend had been deeply impressed by Mohinder's knowledge of Hindu religious philosophy and he viewed him as a superb example of the householder who, later in life, dedicates his life to devotion to the Ultimate Spirit.

Locating Mohinder took the greater part of an hour, driving the gutted alleyways, asking street names over and over, and gleaning information more by deduction than any clear fact of location. Finally we were at the edge of community, where the typical three-storied, close-knit apartments gave way to low, single-story row houses. As with most poor Indian city neighborhoods, the streets and walkways were filled with trash and puddles. The Indian is almost totally imbued with the process of identifying Self with the Universal

Spirit (or some specific manifestation of it) and nearly every-where you will see evidence that each person is immaculate unto himself but has little awareness of his non-self environ-ment. This, too, may have been and may still be a survival tool in a country where the population had already reached 100 million long before Thomas the Apostle ventured there around 4 A.D.

Mohinder's neighborhood was no exception. Debris was scattered everywhere outside, but once you stepped inside the open door onto the smooth slate floor, the interior was nearly antiseptic.

I was asked to have some tea and had no hesitancy at all to sit on the floor by the tiny, low table and drink tea from the plate where it was poured to cool. Mohinder spoke the excellent, literary English so typical of the English taught in Indian schools. His wife and children hovered in an alcove, ready to serve tea as soon as cups emptied. I have experienced life of the Indian poor on many occasions and I always wish that time could stand still while I absorb the glow of love of universe and the fulfillment of just knowing that I have wit-nessed so many times. Mohinder, his wife and children were all totally beatific. There was not a trace of reticence or self-consciousness or of any sense of spiritual presumption. The radiation of an inner peace and joy filled the bare, cool, tiny apartment.

Mohinder was the caretaker of the neighborhood Hindu temple. He had formerly been a government worker and lived on a tiny pension while he and his family kept the temple ready for the constant stream of pujas and special rituals.

The scene was mind-boggling for a pure-bred Westerner. Here was an intellectual, schooled in Indian philosophy
and history, with a magnificently capable mind living at the
edges of poverty, barely clothed and fed, yet deeply and di-
vinely content. I did not know a single intelligent mind living
in such poverty in the U.S. At home intelligence and schooling
are nearly always aimed toward material sufficiency (even
among the religious these days). Only when that is achieved
can one think about such things as the meaning and purpose
of life.

It was a charming visit with Mohinder nonetheless.
There was something about the worn slate floors and the
wash-weary saris of Satwant and the girls, something about the
faded paper pictures of Hindu saints in the otherwise unclut-
tered, sparkling clean apartment. I began to become aware
that the something was a growing feeling of flow and harmony
or, perhaps if description failed me, certainly with a draining
away of disharmony and distraction. This tiny family was so
completely enveloped by its spiritual bond that happiness
swept around it like the halo of the rising sun.

However entranced I was with Mohinder's gentle
philosophizing, I was also aware that my primary mission was
to gather data about the new miracle man, Sai Baba.

Mohinder knew little personally about Baba but he
gave me the lead into one of my more unusual adventures in
India. He told me that the woman who had first taught Sai
Baba, some twenty-five years ago, was now living in Madras,
the next stop on my itinerary. Mohinder supplied the address
of Mati. . . . and, somewhat hesitatingly, told me to go with
caution. I was a bit puzzled, but to be able to interview the

person who had helped Sai Baba get started was too good an opportunity to miss.

Although it was evening when I arrived in Madras a few weeks later, I started immediately for Mati's house. It was dark by the time my taxi found its way to the suburb where Mati lived, and although most of the two and three storied extended family houses glowed dimly with their scanty lighting, at the address of Mati, there was a striking difference. The house was unusually wide, and on one side brightly glowing colored lights were shining behind closed draperies. I was relieved to see the bright lights.

As I stepped up the short walk from the street, I could see tall robed figures moving through the entryway into the closed, brightly lighted room to the right. I pressed the buzzer and within a second the door was answered by an incredibly handsome, elegantly robed, tall young man. I told him I had been sent by Mohinder to see Mati and he admitted me promptly.

With a carefully modulated voice, and with the charming, lilting accent of India, the young man bade me wait while he prepared Mati for my visit. I was left alone in the entryway and my eyes went immediately toward the brightly lighted room. I could see a brilliantly painted altar, extraordinarily beautiful flowers to each side, bright wall hangings and enormous pillows scattered about on the floor. It was obviously a shrine for rich religious ceremony.

Toward the back of the house, through modestly opened doors, I caught glimpses of more robed, tall figures. The robes were brilliantly red, all identical, and, as I got used to the dim light, I became aware that the figures were all surprisingly alike as well. They were all very tall, all beautiful, and all in their mid- to late twenties. But before my thoughts could crystallize, the first young man came back to lead me up the steps to Mati's private apartment on the second floor.

There couldn't have been a greater contrast. In the central room, dead center, was a broad iron bedstead covered with nothing but blue canvas ticking. Her length stretched down the bed with head on hand in the sleeping Buddha position, a popular postural signal of guruhood, Mati lay—in a faded old housedress.

"Well, what do you want," she grunted.

Stunned I was, but somehow I could also appreciate her apparent annoyance. I explained briefly that I was gathering information about the mystic, magic man, Sai Baba.

It was as if I had shot off a revolver. The old lady shifted her position sharply and I felt that she was reloading her artillery. I swear she spit a little, then she snickered and told me to sit. An aide, one of the tall, red-robed young men, brought me a chair while I explained my mission in somewhat greater detail. All the while there were shadowy comings-and-goings of the young male attendants, each moving quickly but silently and with considerable serious intent. I guessed they were preparing for a religious ceremony.

Meanwhile, Mati seemed to be cranking up for a full-blown tirade. There was anger in her eyes as she began her story about Sai Baba. She had "found" him near Puttiparti when he was nearing twelve. She adopted him informally, and since she herself had known samadhi and thus possessed the supernatural powers of enlightenment, she began to instruct him in both religious philosophy and magical practices ("the powers").

The story was, in fact, nothing more than a personalized version of instruction in raja yoga, information I had heard so often I knew it by heart. Mati's discourse choked angrily on the Hindu precept that if one gains supernatural powers during the pursuit of spiritual enlightenment, one *does not* abuse these powers—ever, under any circumstances. To do so is to betray the trust of the spiritual entities that endowed the powers.

Mati would first confirm Sai Baba's powers to create vibhuthi (the holy ash) out of the air, then she would attack him violently for abusing his powers and manufacturing the jewelry he "materialized" for favored (rich) patrons and devotees. Time after time she would swing between praise and condemnation. The boy who became Sai Baba grew up in a religious environment to be sure, but Mati's tale made one suspicious that she herself had perhaps soiled the pureness of the spiritual life. She kept repeating that she had taught him everything he knew, and certainly she had encouraged his use of magical powers.

But all through the scorn, Mati insisted that Sai Baba had, indeed, been born with some supernatural powers. Her venom was thrust at the way he violated the trust of the gods by abusing the powers and using them for material gain. I got the distinct impression that she was more annoyed by her relative lack of wealth than by the "abuse" itself. It was as if there were anyone who had a right to be a magic person, it was Mati.

At the same time I half-consciously began to sort out my impressions, making associations between the scene at Mati's house and the story she was telling me. Mati had said that she "adopted" Sai Baba when he was about twelve and that she had left him (or he her) when he was about twenty-eight. And, well, here we were with Mati and a houseful of elegant young men in their mid-twenties. I wondered whether their bold red robes were a symbol of Mati's brand of Hindu tantra.

Two young men glided into the room and whispered to Mati. She immediately stiffened into a regal pose, waved her hand imperiously and told me the interview was over.

As I left, I tried my best to imprint the vivid display of the altar room into my memory. Actually, I was searching for signs of Tantric Hinduism (not Tantric Buddhism). For those uninitiated in the fine points of Hinduism, the followers of the tantric tradition are those who focus on varieties of sexual activities as the ideal practices for achieving spiritual ecstasy and enlightenment (see also p. 246).

SAI BABA: PART II

However titillating the evening with Mati had been, the only important information about Sai Baba I had gotten was that in all likelihood he was slightly more flim-flam man than guru. It was not until two years later when I was privy to some salty down-to-earth gossip that my views of Sai Baba finally jelled. Even so, what with all that happened on my visit to Sai Baba's ashram in Puttiparti, I should have known the score right then and there.

My chase of Sai Baba now had me in Bangalore in south central India. Of all the cities in India that breathe the air of home, it is Bangalore. It is on higher elevation than the coastal cities and there is much more of the verdant, deciduous foliage about, a crisper climate and fewer weather-stained buildings.

I was exploring life in a real Indian hotel, not a hotel that could also accommodate Westerners. Let me take a moment to describe it, for I doubt if the reader will ever have such an experience (or perhaps me either again for that matter). The hotel itself was in the shape of the old-style American motel—short strings of low bungalows scattered about the grounds and a central eating hall. Each bungalow consisted of a long, wide room with enormously wide screened windows at each end, and bare of furniture except for a row of cots draped with mosquito netting. Period. The only signs of bedding were the ubiquitous blue ticking mattresses on each of the four cots. Since most Indians still carry bedding and most necessities when they travel, strictly Indian hotels do not usually supply sheets, pillows, towels, or toilet paper. The "bathroom" was a fairly large room, some 10 by 10 feet, containing a pipe with tap on one wall and two brightly colored plastic buckets, one large and one small, for bathing and rinsing. The john? Oh yes, there was an open drain with a big tin cup nearby for flushing down the drain.

Just one more note about the hotel. It was "veg," of course, meaning vegetarian, but this offers no hardship since Indian food is almost always delicious with or without meat. Exhausted from travel the evening I registered, I promptly ordered "bed coffee" (my favorite Indian custom) for six the next morning. Right on time the next day the room boy sprang up the cottage steps and burst into the room. He peeled back the mosquito netting and plunked the tray on my lap. It was all warm and wonderful, bright and cheery. The coffee smelled divine and the toast looked marvelous. With an instinctive move, I began to butter the toast. I stared. I was spreading the toast with a great lump of pure white Crisco! Still, it was an awfully good breakfast.

It was not too difficult to arrange for a trip to Puttiparti to see Sai Baba, a trip of a bit more than two hours north of Bangalore by car. After all, pilgrims have been working the Bangalore to Puttiparti route for years.

As I later reconstructed my experience and sorted out my observations, there are several classes of pilgrims to Puttiparti. The most obvious and the most frequent are the wellness seekers (both Indians and Westerners). They will endure the squalor of the village and faithfully attend the twice-daily bajans (bay-jahns, the prayer chanting sessions when Sai Baba makes his appearance) until called for private interviews and healing. There are also large numbers of apparently fairly wealthy native Indian devotees, followed, numerically, by American devotees, and lastly, a scattering of poor native Indians.

For any devotee, rich or poor, in good health or bad, it can be a long and arduous trip to Puttiparti. For me, the adventurer, the drive was enchanting. It was as if you were watching a montage of all India unfold in front of you. We left the tree-lined boulevards of Bangalore, moving through strange mixes of citrus and apple or peach groves, on to endless stone quarries. Even the fences lining the highway were made of granite, curious stone replicas of wooden post and rail fences. Each two dozen miles or so seemed to represent a different subculture.

Finally we turned off on a side road. It was deeply gouged with wheel impressions, ruts that ensured you stayed within its bounds. The scarred road became much more than a road. It seemed like a mechanical trolley pulling the world that was me and all my culture past incredible scenes, as if the landscapes were theatre stages. This sensation was, I suppose, created when the road tried to course through the villages. There were, literally, no edges. The roadside merged with the fronts, backs, or sides of small stone dwellings, and if the houses were built at hit-or-miss angles, so the road squished its way around their obstructions, deepening the ruts into cavernous snares for the unwary. And the entire scene was filthy.

Trash, scraps of cloth, broken beds, old bicycle frames and dung were scattered everywhere. Cow dung patties around houses is no problem; they have been molded for a purpose and have lost their odor. But here in these rural villages, fresh, smelly dung was everywhere and one could see human dung being laid down at the moment. I was surprised since most rural Indians take great care with their toilet, often walking long distances to use the fields, men on one side of town, women on the other. But here, so close to the great guru and magic man, society had become less than primitive. It had become hopeless and hateful.

The wretched scenes were, however, only a prelude to the chaos of poverty in Puttiparti. Literally cheek by jowl as they say, lay the most miserable attempt at community I have ever seen, pressed insistently against the clean, modest, yet inviting buildings in Sai Baba's ashram. The village was, in fact, separated from the ashram by only the rutted dirt road that swelled widely in salute to the ashram. The village was just as mean as those we had just passed through, but one short span had been converted into places of business. Tiny shacks, built from local stone and worn lumber dragged in from the gods know where, had been fashioned into small caricatures of shops with rickety counters where monstrous gold-like medals of Sai Baba were displayed. Some shops featured worn pamphlets and cheap paper pictures of Sai Baba, but most simply tried to sell cheap trinkets plastered with pictures of their living saint. Along the strip of scrungy shops were several equally scrungy eating places that displayed bottles of Coca-Cola to attract attention. Unbelievably two of the places contained a few tables and benches, furniture so rickety that when a group of us sat down, one fellow slid out of the shop when the bench collapsed.

Puttiparti was, in a word, pitiful. Its people were not merely aboriginal or people who had been depressed to below poverty level. They were people who had been neglected not only by the world and by India, but by the man next door.

For Sai Baba lived next door. At the time of my visit, the ashram was being expanded. An enormous open meeting hall the size of a football field was being erected and in its half-finished state it provided shelter for dozens of poor Indian pilgrims. Stretched out along one side of the grounds were modern types of small office-like buildings, one housing the post office and another handling various foodstuffs such as packets of rice and tea. Perpendicular to and along another side was a long series of much older buildings which served as dormitories and eating halls. Both must be very large in India since devotees come to holy places in massive numbers and from great distances. At mealtimes there can be, for example, perhaps sixty or seventy rows each with thirty or fifty seated pilgrims and ashramites with mats or giant banana leaves before them, like clones in a produce market. Ashra-mites serve all the food from huge kettles, swinging the giant pots along the aisles and depositing great servings on each banana leaf without ever missing a beat.

The third side of the ashram village gleamed with the white-washed plaster of new dormitories being built for the wealthier pilgrims. Each ground floor unit consisted of a front room about 6 by 10 feet, and a small square back room for cooking and washing. Off to the side was a real toilet even though the drainage facilities had not been finished. Indeed, the entire population of the ashram used the field in back of the new dormitories. It was not much space for hundreds and hundreds of people and the only recourse a modest Westerner might have would be to use the field facilities at non-peak hours. The other difficulty was the odor. It really did stink unmercifully.

Last is best, they say, and the fourth side of the ashram compound houses Sai Baba, some of his principal attendants and his elephant. Baba's house is strangely like an antebellum mansion of the deep South, complete with an expanse of semi-circular portico in front. Unlike Southern homes, however, parade-blue trim shines along the portico and shutters. Be-tween the elephant's house and Sai Baba's lie the grounds for the bajans. It is here that the devotees sit, men to the right and women to the left and wait for the hour of bajans when Baba will appear. An aide starts the chanting, the familiar chant heard in all ashrams. The sounds are haunting there in the still, warm Indian air, the tones rising and falling gently with great reverence. The expectation of Sai Baba walking through the throngs of devotees is muted by devotion. The women show their anxious hopes by tiny, jerking movements of the legs or yearning movements in the face, but always completely restrained.

Yet, if your ear is tuned to the inner hopes of the waiting devotees, you can hear tension mount in the chanting as the crowd waits for Baba to appear. Then, as the holy man emerges through the doorway a wave of silence spreads to stem the chant. And finally, there he is, the magic man of India, a surprisingly short figure with an Afro haircut. In his orange gown he strides purposefully down the paths, giving the blessing (darshan) to the right and to the left. In a few moments he begins to select petitioners for private interviews and one can hear muted gasps and sighs throughout the crowd. At the same time Baba begins the mystical magic of the vibhuthi, the holy ash. With a lightning sweep of his bare arm he reaches into the air and pulls down a handful of gray ash. He scans the rows of petitioners and here and there places the gift of vibhuthi in outstretched hands. Then suddenly darshan ends. Baba strides toward his palace while the favored few are shepherded around to the back to wait their turn for special favors. The rest rise and quietly disperse, somewhat bewildered and at a loss for what to do until the next bajan. A few become genuinely alarmed.

I remember, for instance, an exquisitely handsome couple named Jim and Dolly. Jim was afflicted by an eye disease that was rapidly causing blindness. They believed deeply that Sai Baba could cure Jim if only Jim could be selected for private interview and a healing touch. The year before in the U.S. they had shared a vision that Sai Baba was to be their savior. They sold all their possessions to come to

Puttiparti, buying a small truck-like car in Madras that they lived in here at the ashram. They had now been here for three weeks, patient at the twice-daily bajans, waiting for Sai Baba's special glance. They had petitioned Baba with notes, calls to his house, and begging help from Baba's favored devotees like my hostess. For twenty-one days Baba had given them no sign. And all the time Jim's vision worsened. As we left this particular bajan, I heard them quietly crying in despair.

"How much longer should we try?" was Dolly's worried question.

Jim hugged Dolly half for her caring support, half in longing for understanding and love.

"If I felt better, I would stay," I heard Jim say, "but now I am so worn out with waiting and hurt, that I just want to lie down and sleep forever."

With infinite gentleness and quiet tears they helped each other into the truck. By evening they were gone.

SAI BABA:
PART III

I am well known for an indomitable will. I had heard rumors about Sai Baba's flightiness and head-strong behavior many times. He was reputed to be infuriatingly elusive. If he had an important appointment in, say, Madras, he could possibly be found instead in Whitefield or Bangalore or in Puttiparti. He seemed to love his mischief and the chase although when he was to appear at religious rallys, he was always visible to the millions—but rarely available personally. What made me think I could best him in an encounter of the wills, I'll never know, but I certainly came close to winning, and perhaps did score a kind of victory.

Because of Sai Baba's reputed wiliness and the rumors about how he could cleverly avoid interviews by Western journalists and scientists, I took the precaution of setting up a special introduction.

It wasn't the best insurance in the world, but my friend Kanak in Calcutta had been a personal friend of Sai Baba's agent (or PR man) before this man had decided to attend Sai Baba full time. Kanak sent a telegram to this man about my arrival asking that he take special care of me. Surprisingly, because of the notorious unreliability of the Indian Telex system, Kanak received a reply. This assured her that Sai Baba would be delighted to talk with me and I was to be his guest at the ashram.

I was naively expectant. At the ashram gate my driver found a messenger and after some fifteen minutes down the walk swung a tall Indian in pure white cotton robes. It was Baba's special attendant. He was all smiles as he greeted me. He apologized for the wait, greeted me in the name of the ashram, and took me on a tour of the grounds. With considerable hospitality he guided me to one of the ground floor mini-suites, depositing me into the hands of a well-fed, pink and white sari'd American lady. She was to be my "hostess" and guide, and the PR man left saying that all was arranged for me to meet with Sai Baba after the morning's bajan.

Indeed!

My hostess literally effused. Whether I commented on how nice her ashram room was or on her beautifully sheer pink floral sari or how large the grounds were, she responded with a stream of superlatives. She showed me, much too intimately, how to use the bathroom facilities of the field, unpacked a giant suitcase loaded with exquisite saris, and hidden below them, a score of bottled water and orange juice containers and jars of coffee. She confessed that she had "sneaked into town" (pshaw! the nearest "town" with such supplies was

Bangalore, more than two hours away and odds were that such purchases could be made only in Madras where neighboring villages produce the finest of sari silk).

A few elegantly clad Indian ladies stopped by, the signal for us all to start for the morning ritual with Sai Baba. (Later I searched for duplicates of some of the exquisite sari material and found they cost many hundreds of dollars.)

I confess it was exciting, that first bajan. I was eager to be caught up in the chanting, to wait expectantly for Baba. Magically the crowd settled into set patterns, leaving wide walkways for their guru. I've already described the feeling of the crowd—an extraordinary quiet discipline in the presence of their superstar. No one grasped for his gown, no one cried out his misery, no one shouted for attention. The sole display of the petitioners' urgency and desperate need was the outstretched hands waiting for vibhuthi. And equally as remarkable, there were no cries about being left out or overlooked. Life is eternal in the Hindu view.

As a special visitor, I was given a spot in a row next to the walkway. I stretched my arm and cupped my palm, ready to receive the holy ash as Sai Baba passed by. Trying to catch his eye for personal attention, I noticed how strangely he held his glance to some focus in mid-space, looking neither at the sitting devotees below nor off into the distance. He did, however, deposit a good supply of holy ash in my hand, and I swear he was fully aware of who I was and what my mission was. I recklessly spoiled the hush of the ritual and spoke up clearly.

"I've come a long way to see you," was all I could get out before he swept onward. Of course there was no response, and I knew also that nearly everyone had come a long way. Yet I knew he knew about me.

The morning ritual was over as quietly as it had begun. I was puzzled that I had not been selected for a private interview. My hostess seemed to be amused. A smug kind of manner took over. She said she would find the PR man and get the time of my interview with Baba. Then she added coyly that no one could ever leave the ashram without Baba's permission.

Nearing a smirk, she tacked on a teasing line, "No one would dream of leaving here without Baba's permission. Anyone who ever did met with disaster."

It was a threat I was to hear all afternoon and evening.

Two nearby young Western women took over the task of coping with me. One, a boyish young lady appropriately named Timmy, told how she had been visited by Sai Baba in the middle of a dream one night as she slept in her room in Palo Alto. She was a graduate student in zoology and obviously very bright. She accepted the reality of Sai Baba's teleporting himself around the world and described how the holy man woke her from her dream and beckoned her to Puttiparti. The very next day she packed her things, simply left her home and started for India. It had been a difficult trip but two weeks later, here she was, bedroll and all, ecstatic with love for everything that meant Sai Baba.

My hostess had disappeared, and as my new acquaintances searched for her, it was becoming clear that any interview with Sai Baba was being put off until later in the day.

We decided to go to lunch in the village (insanity to think of eating in the village filth but there isn't a whole lot to do in an ashram). There were now Timmy, Jim (the boy going blind), his girl Dolly, myself, a silent European man, and an exotic, beautiful woman named Angel. She told me she had just completed touring with Ravi Shankar and that from time to time she came to Sai Baba for spiritual replenishment. It was a strangish group.

Angel was a joy, gay and lilting, with the kind of wholly outgoing happiness that most of us do not find in most somber seekers of the spirit. Her home was in London and I was sorry to learn that she would be leaving in a few hours to start the trip home. Angel had been in India with Indians long enough to know how to handle even the sorriest of conditions. I was not yet at that stage, and as we walked down Puttiparti's dusty street, the stark poverty stabbed my heart. Small children with bowed legs and pot bellies, children unwashed for months, children in rags so tattered my mechanic wouldn't use them, children everywhere here in Puttiparti could not be in more miserable conditions. Nor were the children the only sufferers. The adults, too, were in tattered clothes, their sandals tied with stray bits of string, their hair matted, their bodies streaked with layers of dirt.

The weather was sultry and the flies, ladened with moisture, could scarcely move from bits of crumb to the edges of Coke bottles. Flies were everywhere, on the heads of the shop keepers, on women's clothes and children's lips. Only my curiosity let me sit in the eating shack. Angel and Dolly, unaffected by the squalor, ordered cooked food for us all, and although I watched the cook use a filthy rag to scrape the skillet, I sampled the food. It was, not surprisingly, awful.

Back in the ashram grounds I searched everywhere for my "hostess" and the PR man. No one would help me. My new acquaintances led me on another tour of the ashram and chattered endlessly about how clever Baba was, how you must always be completely obedient to your guru, and how you could not leave the ashram without Baba's permission. Slowly my unconscious began to process the message; only slowly did it come into consciousness.

Somewhere along the line we discovered that the afternoon bajans were to start early because Baba was going to show off his elephant. (Every self-respecting swami in India has his own personal elephant.) My new friends went off to nap and I kept wandering about. There was absolutely no one who seemed to be in charge of anything. I distinctly felt a conspiracy coming on.

I gave up my search for help and took a rest in my hostess's room. She finally came in, made cool drinks from the bottled water and surprised me by saying that it was all arranged for me to see Baba right after the afternoon bajans.

Mid-afternoon we all trooped over to the bajan grounds and settled ourselves down for a double-feature. And it was a nice elephant show. Baba's elephant was a young, sleek Indian specimen, too young to know the many tricks most swamis enjoy, but it was friendly and seemed to love the audience. Sai Baba was gentle with him and let him steal the show. Then Baba took over—briefly. He made a quick swing around the men's side of the waiting devotees and disappeared into his house. I looked to my hostess, and sure enough, even though I had not been tapped for a private interview, she led me to the back of Baba's house. We entered a small storeroom-like affair packed with great burlap sacks of rice and other grains. In a back corner there was a stairway to the second floor.

For the next hour I waited patiently while my hostess scurried hither and yon, presumably working to fit me into Sai Baba's schedule. About every ten minutes she would caution me that I should plan to spend the night with her, then I could see Baba at leisure the next day. Her campaign to make me stay gathered steam as she would first try to entice me with how cozy the evening recreations with various devotees would be, then as I protested, she would threaten me with the direst of consequences should I leave the ashram without Baba's permission. Permission to leave, of course, could be granted only by Baba personally.

Well, you don't threaten a willful, independent woman, and my ire began to rise as delay followed delay and the threats became more explicit. I was tired and hungry and worried about appointments in Bangalore the next day. Besides, it was getting dark and it was a long drive back to Bangalore. I decided to give the experience another hour and then leave. I was becoming convinced it was all a run-around and, too, I remembered Jim and Dolly's twenty-one day wait for Baba's attention to a very serious problem.

Someone led me back to my hostess's quarters to get my money, notes and travel clothes. The door was locked. I asked my driver, waiting nearby, to send someone to find the lady while I collapsed on the concrete steps. Finally, through the fading light, I saw my hostess bouncing down the path, her arms loaded with bedding.

"Baba says you must stay," she announced. "I think we can get the interview done tomorrow."

Adrenalin surged through my veins. With undisguised annoyance I said I had to leave no matter what Baba said, and would my hostess kindly unlock her room door so I could get my belongings that had been left there for safe-keeping.

My hostess plunked herself down beside me, laughing wickedly, giggling her news bulletin:

"I can't find my key," she said, "I've looked everywhere. I thought it was in my purse, but it's gone now."

"Look again," I demanded.

As if the whole thing were a big joke, she began to tackle the huge carpet bag that was her purse. I watched closely as she shuffled her hands through the mass of junk in her purse. Then I saw it—she was palming the key! I grabbed her wrist, bounced it sharply on my knee, and . . . out spat the key.

As I flung my possessions into the car, my former hostess harangued me with screams of vengeance.

"Disaster will strike. Baba has not given you permission to leave. Baba will teach you to obey him. Something terrible will happen to you before you leave India!"

She was still shouting warnings of impending disaster as we drove out of the ashram grounds into the darkness. I had not once taken the threats seriously, but it was an intensely dark night and I was alone, hours away from civilization, in a car with a driver I didn't know. I asked him whether the threats bothered him.

"No, lady," he seemed to chuckle, "Baba only wants to do good things. He gives us schools and helps to educate the poor, and his institutes and ashrams give us all work. I think that perhaps the foreign ladies want to get control of Baba's devotees here at the ashram and have everything their way."

A typical Indian diplomat, I thought. It is a rare Indian that will ever say a harsh word against even the least or rascally of gurus. It is difficult for us Americans to maintain such states of suspended judgment, but this ability is, I think, a mark of the enlightened mind. The swami who exploits or cheats is just as much a part of the universal spirit as anyone else.

Did any disaster befall me? You be the judge.

Two days later I was in the Bangalore airport waiting for a delayed flight that would take me to Bombay for a connecting flight to Nairobi. The airport wait was actually relaxing. It was one of the few (probably the only) airport in India that was truly pleasant. Sunlight streamed in the rows of windows, the seats were comfortable and plentiful, and I was half-drowsing. At the call to board the plane, I gathered my many parcels together, found an excellent seat toward the front of the aircraft, settled in, then suddenly became aware of something missing. Oh God, my good camera was gone.

Despite a search of the airport and plane and despite telexes back and forth to Bombay for airline help, the camera was gone. It was naturally, the expensive one, my cheap backup was still in my hand luggage. And here I was, all set for photography on African safaris.

One of the airport employees told me that the local thieves had become expert in purloining cameras, tape recorders, and other goodies from wealthy patrons that came to visit Sai Baba. He gave me some hope that because the thieves were known, I would get my camera back if I could make it worth his while. I gave him some money and promised more if he could get the camera sent by courier to Nairobi. I never got the camera, of course, and I can only guess that a higher bidder came on the scene. Whoever had taken my camera had done so masterfully. I had not felt a thing when it was slipped from my shoulder.

Naturally I speculated on just how much Sai Baba's influence counted, either supernaturally or via some kind of unofficially appended group that indulged in stolen goods. The thought still intrudes over the years because of the unusual flight to Nairobi.

It was a spectacular flight. First, it was delayed until the next morning. I welcomed the rest, and early the next day we were escorted through customs and boarded a large DC-10 that was surprisingly only half-full. I should have suspected something then, but I was too delighted by all the space available. I read, I rested, made tons of notes and reconciled myself to living with my cheap camera. Finally I began to check the time. Whoa, I thought, we should be nearing Nairobi by now, and there is no land in sight. What's going on?

I queried the young women cabin attendants. If you think Orientals are enigmatic, you haven't encountered the Indian airline attendant. The girls are never told anything. Obviously they are not much help in answering questions such as "when do we get to the airport?". I kept urging the girls to ask the Captain and they would disappear into the control cabin and return saying they didn't know. But smiling sweetly, as usual.

Finally, long after we had been due in Nairobi, the Captain came on the intercom.

"Ladies and gentlemen, we will be landing soon on Mauritius. We are delivering a DC-10 engine to a disabled plane. You can see the engine, strapped to our wing on the right. As soon as the engine is removed, we'll be on our way to Nairobi."

How could I have missed it! There on the right wing were *three* engines, not just the normal two as on the left wing. And of course the lighter passenger load could account for the difference in weight of the engine.

I looked at the map. And stared! We were taking a 2500 mile detour and no one had told anyone anything. We were midway between India and Africa, nowhere near Kenya!

Truthfully, I had always wanted to visit an island like Mauritius but felt I could probably never afford it. As we circled for the landing, beautifully low so that we could see every detail of countryside and village, I was ecstatic. It was like a color picture book of well-groomed English countrysides. There were the gently sloping fields of grain, the rough stone walls, the thatched cottages, and all surrounded by the sea-green ocean softly lapping on the shores.

Structurally the airport was most pleasant. Its biggest drawback was lack of food and drink. Mauritius is well known for its gorgeous stamps, and there was no lack of stamps to buy. But Coca-Cola was all that was available to ease our thirst. And the good gendarmes in charge refused to allow anyone out of the airport. It would be just a few minutes, they said, until the engine was removed from our plane and the flight would be under way.

It wasn't. Not that hour nor the next. We finally learned that the threads on the giant screws holding the engine to the airplane's wing had broken and there was no way they could get the engine off until a crew came with special equipment. It became an agonizing few hours. We could see the non-progress on the plane and all of us were hot and thirsty and the Coke supply had become as warm as the airport.

An elderly Indian couple was sitting a few aisles away and I had been watching the husband as he wandered about in an agitated fashion. Soon he approached me. "My wife does not feel well," he said, "and we only have Indian money, so we cannot buy Coca-Cola. Would it be possible for you to give me an American dime so I can get her a drink?" (Indian money is totally worthless outside of India.)

Over the man's resistance I persuaded him to take a dollar (which he could change there). He seemed nearly in tears and begged me for my name and address so he could send me a thank you letter. With some reluctance, I gave it to him. He told me he was a tea planter in Kenya. I watched him and his wife settle into greater comfort with a cluster of drinks. Some four months later I received two *pounds* of Kenyan tea by sea mail. Do you know how much two pounds of tea is? It's enough for the entire British army!

Some five hours after landing on Mauritius we were under way to Nairobi. It was, perhaps, four in the afternoon. I had learned we were to cross Madagascar and was eager to see it. Most people don't realize how much one can learn about a country from an air view. But the skies were darkening and soon we were surrounded by enormous black clouds. And then, like volcanoes in the sky, the clouds were split by enormous chasms of red and orange with deep purple rivulets cascading down to the sea. One could see giant streaks of lightning and hear the enormous roar of thunder over the aircraft's engines. It was, in a way, terrifying, but the spectacle was so great and so awesome that one knew immediately the scenes were worth the risk. My trusty little tourist camera served me well and I still preserve the pictures of the cataclysm in the sky.

Then, almost as quickly as it had begun, the storm was over. I could see we were over land. The sky was navy blue and the stars glowed as they can glow only in the other hemisphere. We landed smoothly in Nairobi, and as we trooped from the plane to the airport buildings, I looked up at the expanded sky, blew a kiss to the glistening stars and wondered what Sai Baba was doing then.

I don't know who really won the battle of the wills. I lost my prize camera, an expensive disaster to be sure, and perhaps by Baba's curse. But there was another side to the ledger. I had been gifted by the inspiring sights of Mauritius, experienced an unforgettably exquisite storm over Madagascar, and eventually received two pounds of Kenyan tea. These were gifts for the mind and spirit and psyche. Did Sai Baba deal only with material gifts or material retribution? Why would a holy man wish disaster to befall a visitor? Certainly demanding obedience from non-devotees would not be worthy of a guru whose enlightenment assumed non-attachment and rejection of ego. I decided that my mind gifts were much more valuable than even the best of cameras. I wondered if Baba were happy.

SAI BABA: EPILOGUE

The most sensational miracle Sai Baba ever wrought was his thrice raising from the dead of J.C. Collins (a pseudonym). It had been widely rumored that Baba had revived a number of dying people, but the J.C. Collins story was told and retold with the greatest of awe and wonder.

While I profess to be intensely skeptical about psychic phenomena, somehow the world conspires to make me privy to scores of minor miracles. I was just beginning my quest of the Sai Baba story and in line to register at the Taj on a beautifully sunny day in Bombay when I heard the desk clerk say, "A bell man will show you to your room, Mr. Collins."

I stared and sure enough it was J.C. Collins, the man three times resurrected from the dead by Sai Baba! I charged between Collins and his wife and excitedly begged for an interview. The Collinses were kind and we spent some three hours going over the Sai Baba miracles. The following account was told to me first hand.

It seems that Mr. Collins and his wife were relaxing one evening in their California home when J.C. suffered a sudden heart attack. By quick action the ambulance arrived in minutes, and with the Collinses safe inside, sped on its way to the hospital. The paramedic noted the absence of pulse and respiration and began taking the proper emergency measures. Collins later reported that he was suddenly grasped by Baba, shaken into consciousness and comforted while Baba quietly assured him that all would be well.

The paramedic was stunned. His dying patient was suddenly sitting up, brushing aside the emergency equipment, and acting for all the world like someone truly risen from the dead into vigorous good health. Mrs. Collins was holding her husband in her arms, repeating aloud,

"Baba was here. Baba has made you well. Baba came when I called. I called to Baba and he came. I saw him shake you and tell you everything would be all right."

J.C. was in delirious confusion. Long a Baba devotee, he didn't know whether to pray his thanks to Baba first or confirm the miracle his wife had witnessed to both his wife and the startled paramedic. He tried to do both, at the same time shaking off the paramedic's efforts to administer to him. By the time the ambulance had reached the hospital, J.C. had decided he owed it to the medics to at least stay in the hospital overnight and be examined no matter how fine he felt at the moment. The paramedic turned J.C. over to the emergency staff and went off to rehash the whole affair with the driver. The driver was his witness that J.C. was virtually dead when they loaded him into the ambulance. On the other hand, the driver also had witnessed J.C.'s fine fettle when they took him out of the ambulance.

Naturally J.C. and his wife were shaken and fatigued. The medical staff persuaded J.C. to suffer all the tubes and wires of intensive care while the hospital arranged for a cot for Mrs. Collins in J.C.'s room and finally everyone left them alone. They oh'ed and ah'ed over the miracle for a while then dozed off.

In the eerie hours of early morning, just before the dawn, J.C.'s heart failed him again. The cardiac monitor in the nurse's station sounded its alarm, the nurse gave the commands for the emergency team and dashed for J.C.'s room. There was J.C., half sitting up in bed, his wife at his side, and both engaged in conversation with a shadowy figure half-seated at the end of the bed.

J.C. never explained what the nurse thought or what the emergency team did. All he could remember was that he had had a suffocating feeling and had called out for Baba. Within the second, he had felt Baba's presence and was instantly well. The medics were suitably astounded.

It did not take much thought for the Collinses to decide that if Baba could come to California to save J.C. it would be much more convenient (and safer, too) if they went to someplace closer to Baba. As soon as J.C. convinced his medics he was all right, the Collinses departed for India. Their first stopover was Madras, and no sooner were they in their hotel when J.C. went down again with what seemed to be his third heart attack. Then, almost as soon as he had been put into the ambulance, Baba was by his side, comforting him and telling him that he was not to die this time. A week later the Collinses were at the ashram where, in a warm welcoming ceremony, Baba materialized a pair of golden wedding rings to celebrate their faith and renewal.

It is, perhaps, a special phenomenon of Sai Baba that his miracles and healing powers have remained within certain peculiar limits. Of the Westerners Baba has attracted, a few have a strong commitment to his ministry while others have drifted off into TM or embraced other gurus. Still, for the ordinary Indian, Baba is a true miracle man, a worthy successor to Satya Sai Baba of Shirdi, the quiet mystic who was universally revered.

There have been books about Sai Baba circulated in the United States, and about Baba and the Collinses, but there has never been the dramatic adulation for Sai Baba by the Western world that swamis such as Mukdananda or Rajneesh or the Maharishi have commanded. On the other hand, these swamis have attracted relatively few of the average kind of Indian while Baba commands millions of Indian devotees. Does the Indian innately discriminate the spiritual from the not-so-spiritual or can Westerners not see beyond the veils of appearance? Or is it just the opposite, that the Indian, with the Hindu convictions about "the powers" and the illusory nature of the physical world (maya) is the victim of magic while the Westerner more often finds a surfeit of miracles unbelievable?

Or is it all of the above?

TERRORIST
INDIA

The strangest, most soul-shattering experience of my Indian adventures was a very personal introduction to the barbarism and terrorism that can erupt so unexpectedly in India. It all began abruptly but was handled with typical Indian gentleness and moved with an excruciating slowness that marks India's historic philosophic passivity and how completely individual welfare is sacrificed in gain for the spirit of all generations.

It was in the early days of biofeedback and the occasion of an uncommon meeting between the foremost pioneer of biofeedback (me) and a prominent Indian biomedical engineer in one of India's most prestigious scientific universities. When I had revealed my plans to visit Dr. Ex, my Indian friends raised their eyebrows in surprise. Had I heard, they asked, of the notorious swami, P.R. Sarkar, head of the

Ananda Marg? "Vaguely," I had answered, at which I was promptly informed how gossip was spreading that Dr. Ex was one of his devotees.

In the cutesy, superficial gossip of the scientific intelligentsia, it was rumored that this well-known scientist had embraced the political philosophy of a religious cult devoted to terrorism. I sought expert advice in Bombay and was told that Dr. Ex was suspected of holding high office in the Ananda Marg. The Ananda Marg, it turned out, apparently consisted of two very different groups, one serving as a cover for the other. For innocent searchers for spiritual growth it was a semi-religious group; for the Indian Secret Service it was a cover for Indian fascist activities. I was, moreover, told that the leader of the cult, Prabhat Ranjan Sarkar (also known as Anandmurti), was in jail because the police had found the bodies of 16 former cult members buried in the ashram grounds. It was common gossip that once one became a member of the cult, one never left it alive.

My suspect scientist was on the faculty of the Indian Institute of Technology (Madras) and he was leading a number of younger staff and graduate students in a study of the use of alpha brainwave biofeedback in the treatment of epilepsy. Fortunately, one of the Ph.D. candidates, young Abhijit, was the son-in-law of an Indian friend, and so it was that Shireen and I found ourselves in a taxi driving through the vast grounds of the University.

The campus spoke eloquently of the Indian reverence for life and nature. Buildings were separated by acres of rambling, stunted, untended natural growth, sometimes a half mile or so between buildings where deer could be seen grazing. We found the Special Engineering building and the office of Dr. Ex. It could have been designed from a photograph of an ancient British laboratory and smelled as musty as it looked. I settled into my interview with Dr. Ex with my heart pounding as I anticipated my final question about his chosen spiritual guide. I was stuttery by the time I finally asked the question.

His answer stunned me. "My guru is Swami Prabhat Ranjan Sarkar," he announced much as if he were introducing the Prime Minister of India herself. "Baba is the greatest guru in all of India, and I am proud to be his servant."

"If you are really interested in the Ananda Marg," he continued, "I can arrange for us all to meet later this afternoon for tea at my apartment."

I leaped at the chance, and at about 4:30, after more tours of labs and areas of the campus, we participants began to arrive at Dr. Ex's spacious, open, second-story apartment on campus. Dr. Ex's wife greeted us and I was surprised to see that she was the essence of movie stereotyped Aryanism—blonde and blue-eyed, stiff and straight, and an unmistakable German accent. Already in the apartment were one junior staff member and two graduate students, all of whom I soon came to know well.

Mrs. Ex disappeared into the bedroom and I could hear an animated, whispered conversation. The host was in the kitchen, readying tea and lemonade, yet there was a distinct uneasiness among the group waiting in the living room. Their body language spoke clearly of tension and concern. Suddenly there was a rustle and an echo of marching boots, and into the room strode Mrs. Ex accompanied by a bustling, saffron-robed swami. He swished purposively to a large wooden chair positioned between two doorways and seated himself regally upon his throne.

This was Swami Z, second in command to the head guru. His bearing was so impressive, I was surprised when I realized how very small he was. No more than 5 foot 4, I thought. And slender. But oh, so very tough.

Dr. Ex stunned me more by a sudden non sequitur. "Unfortunately you can't meet our guru. Sri Swami Sarkar is currently in jail."

He went on. "But you do know about the Ananda Marg, don't you?"

I nodded. Actually I only knew the United States version—that the Ananda Marg (the Way of Bliss) was a particular spiritual cult that practiced meditation by means of certain asanas (meditative postures). It all seemed very spiritual and healthful. I had, however, been puzzled when I read how the practitioners were organized. One official handbook indicated that ideally Ananda Marg groups should be six or eight and no more than ten. How strange, I thought, it's like the communist cells in the old days. And for some time that may have been truer than I ever cared to admit.

I tried to get a discussion going on meditation techniques, but the atmosphere in the apartment was so charged it was as if the Swami and Dr. Ex were driving toward some preselected topic and no one was cooperating. The young men of the department were fidgeting silently.

Again Dr. Ex came out with a irrelevant remark.

"Would you like to become a member of the Ananda Marg?" he asked without any preface.

I felt the adrenalin jerk me to excitement. What an adventure it would be! To be inducted into what apparently was a very powerful branch of the Ananda Marg, and to be with such electrifying Indians would be mind-blowing. My intellectual curiosity caught on fire. I had to know more. Did they have any books, I asked.

My interest was so genuine the two Exes and the swami retired to the bedroom for consultation. Dr. Ex stuck his head out to report, "We do have a book, but you would have to read it here."

That wasn't reasonable, I argued, because I would have no time to study the material. They parleyed again. This time Dr. Ex told me that they would have Abhijit bring the book to my hotel that night and he would pick it up in the morning. The arrangement seemed a bit strange. Then Dr. Ex asked if we could give Swami a lift into town.

Swami Z insisted on sitting next to me in the taxi and it was as if steel rods were pressed against me. He craned his tan head around to face me and let fly with a commercial for the Ananda Marg that any of the networks would have been proud of. When was I leaving Madras? When was I returning? Too long—I must join the group within the week. He would not let me go. I must be with them. He would see to that.

I was feeling panicked. The day was cool but I was sweating by the time he left the cab. He promised he would come to get me the next afternoon and would arrange for me to be inducted into his cult.

Later, at the hotel, Abhijit arrived with the book. He had pedaled fully ten miles and would have to repeat the trip the next morning to pick up the book to return it to the swami.

It was obviously a highly revered book, requiring special care. I couldn't wait to dig into it.

Thirty minutes later I was shaking with horror and revulsion. Sarkar wrote that the whole world had degenerated and he had been called to establish a new order called sadvipra, a world government he alone designed. He admonished his followers they might have to resort to physical violence. I read how expedient it was to murder your enemies, how profitable it was to terrorize the countryside, how necessary it was to slay the communists, how soon it would be that the Ananda Marg could overthrow—not just the Indian government, but other leftist, socialist governments of the world—and surprisingly, including the government of the U.S.

It was *Mein Kampf* all over again and worse.

And Swami Z was coming to get me the next day! Shireen and I made plans to move on—quickly. Early the next morning we called Abhijit to say the book would be at the hotel desk, then hired a car and driver to explore the countryside returning to Madras only in time to be at the airport for a flight we had already booked to Sri Lanka.

We were not the only ones to flee. Within the week Dr. Ex disappeared. As if by magic everything in his apartment and office was gone. No one seemed to know anything. It was young Abhijit who got the scare. The day after the mysterious disappearance, as Abhijit was leaving for the lab, he heard a car pull up outside. Answering a knock at the door, he came face to face with the police. There was a warrant for Dr. Ex's arrest. The police did not explain the warrant. It may have been for the ashram problems or for the terrorist activities. None of us would ever know.

A month later, back in Los Angeles, a casual visitor to my lab asked me if I knew about the secret biofeedback research being conducted at Ames Air Force Base outside of San Francisco. He showed me a small publication from the base, and there—in amongst the research personnel was the name of Dr. Ex—a full fledged consultant to the U.S. Air Force.

Like a good countryman, I called the CIA. No, they had never heard of the Ananda Marg, no, it wasn't on their list of subversive groups, no, they had no information about Indian terrorists. I've had some contact with the CIA over the years, and I was convinced it was becoming less and less well informed.

Two years later I had occasion to query Indira Gandhi about the Ananda Marg. She felt that it was no longer a political force in India (confirming that it *had* been). That same year Sarkar was released from jail and the charges of murdering his ashramites were dropped.

Historically, Indira was probably right. Radicals and terrorists, smugglers and bandits, revolutionaries and missionaries come and go in India, but eventually they all become absorbed in the giant spiritual net that is India. Incidentally, I mean no disrespect in calling Mrs. Gandhi "Indira." Everyone in India called her Indira.

What shocked me was reading the *Los Angeles Times* report (August 26, 1978) on the release of P.R. Sarkar from prison following several trials. P.R. Sarkar is, of course, the head of the Ananda Marg, the swami accused of murder. The prosecution contended that Sarkar "was a power-hungry leader of what it called a subversive organization." the *L.A. Times* article noted, "Ananda Marg, which means 'path of bliss' was founded by Sarkar in 1955 and aims to help individual spiritual growth through meditation, and its 2000 members in the United States also engage in a host of social service activities, including disaster relief and food projects." The *Times* concluded, "For the movement's followers in the United States and 70 other nations where it is established, Sarkar's release means the sect can now go on about its business of meditating and social service."

Indeed!

TIRUPATI

The intrinsic, transcendent wonders of India are rarely discovered by Westerners. The casual visitor or the tourist who must "do" India sees only masses of dusty brown bodies swarming through busy streets to and from labor that scarcely pays a living wage, makes visits to stained and crumbling ancient temples, spends precious hours giggling over sexual statuary and turns livid over the bureaucratic inefficiency of the airlines and hotels. The few visitors who stay a year or two or three every day experience new and constantly enveloping challenges to Western logic and learning. It is only after long months or years of reflection that one begins to appreciate the extraordinary psychic coherence that underlies the Indian spirit and links its great diversity into the appearance of a single entity, India. And while we non-Indians can come to a genuine appreciation of the mind that is India, none of us will ever claim to understand it.

The real mystery of India is, perhaps, how its majority can support a thousand sects and cults with unflagging respect for each, how its most brilliant and cosmopolitan minds can cling so tenaciously to what we Westerners see as myths and superstition. Our social and academic critics often ridicule the practices of India's most brilliant leaders, practices such as Morarji Desai's, the Prime Minister following Mrs. Gandhi, who daily drank his own urine, or ridicule Indira herself for her alleged reliance on half a dozen gurus some of whom seemed to be anything but wise. These same pundits and social critics raise no voice against believers in Oral Roberts or the millions whose earnings go to build Crystal Cathedrals. Yet learning to understand the differences between appearances and reality is, I think, the key to a meaningful appreciation of the mind of India. It is said that when one can see beyond the material forms of our worlds and how feeble their attendant philosophies really are, it is then the paradoxes in India lose their incongruities and become understandable.

The West looks on India as a single, homogeneous entity; she is, in fact, a boiling, churning jumble of clans and bloodline subsets and wide-ranging subjective and intellectual experiences, all held together by the psychic glue of the Hindu understanding of the meaning of life. Internally, India is truly a land of contrasts. One of the most notable contrasts is between the apparent domination of intellectualism to the north in Bengal and the apparent domination of spirituality in India's southeast. Both north and south of the ancient southern capital of Madras there are scores of small ashrams, dozens of Hindu cults, hundreds of temples and endless religious festivals and processions.

In a region with such great religious fervor, one could easily expect to find one of the most revered temples in India. Here, resting on Tirumala Hill just outside Tirupati, is one of the most popular religious shrines in all India, the Lord Venkateswara temple. Not until recently have Westerners been able to visit the temple, and still today, non-Hindus are not permitted to go into the inner shrine, unless, of course, they have either political clout or lots of money to donate or manage to deceive the temple guardians. I suspect all three influences made my visit possible. The Venkateswara temple at Tirupati has become the repository for all the gold and gems its millions of worshippers can bring. It is estimated that ten million dollars in gold and gems is accumulated *per year* from the pilgrims who give the temple deity every ounce of jewelry or gold they have. The poor and the rich, the untouchables and the Brahmins, the abysmally ignorant and the most brilliant, sophisticated Indians all give their worldly wealth to the deity.

I was fortunate to be with three prominent, well-connected Indian ladies on a pilgrimage to pay their respects to Lord Venkateswara in Tirupati. Tirupati is in rural India, some hundred miles northwest of Madras and not easily approachable by plane or train. That is, the trains and planes arrive and leave only once a day, making connections difficult and erratic. The transports arrive in Tirupati in late afternoon and leave in the morning, Indian logic being that devotees will want to spend a full day in and around the temple. These schedules, of course, mean that pilgrims must spend at least two nights in Tirupati, mostly along the roads or in the fields. To circumvent the inconvenient train schedule, our small group hired a car and driver and set out in early morning from Madras.

Tirupati itself lies in a large fertile plain dotted with a few hills toward the west. The tallest is Tirumala and atop it is the Lord Venkateswara temple. The high plateau is large enough to house an entire village but there are only bare fields, well-used, dusty parking areas for the buses and a scattering of buildings all associated with the temple. I estimated that it was at least seven miles up the sprawling hillside to the top and I could understand why modern pilgrims came to the shrine by bus. Still, there were many pilgrims determinedly but wearily marching up the hill.

Although my friends had been concerned that we should arrive early, ahead of the rush of pilgrims, there were, in fact, few pilgrims there so early. I began to realize that we were in a waiting area where we would be approved (or not) to enter the temple. We waited in what looked like an ancient Greek open-air marketplace with benches, and indeed, pilgrims did begin to join us in the wait to be certified for entrance into the temple. In the distance I could see buses arriving with hundreds, perhaps thousands, of pilgrims. We would soon be overwhelmed, I thought.

Finally a briskly moving official came to collect us and move us to the next station where we were to remove our shoes and be certified as Hindus. After another hour's wait, the great gates of the temple suddenly opened and a surge of humanity swept into the antechamber. We were thrust violently forward as the throng rushed into the small, one-way passage. The smell of incense and smoke from the oil lamps was suffocating. It was dark even as the candles flickered and smoked and we were pushed past the dim figures of a score of lesser deities. After some hundred feet we came to a cavernous end where the deity was enthroned. Oil lamps made the scene glow incandescently. I looked. The deity was black!

Yes, the deity was black. I knew it would be, of course, but in a land of a thousand sand-colored deities, one wholly black statue seems to jolt the physical homogeneity of the Hindu pantheon. On the shoulders of the statue were garlands of flowers while gems and bits of gold were scattered about in front of the shrine. The crowd pushed us on, and we had but a scant second to view the deity. The pilgrims were alternately sighing with admiration or softly uttering bits of prayers and chants as they offered their gold and jewels and flowers. We were pushed on and literally squeezed out of the temple. Outside, huge throngs were waiting their turn to enter the temple.

To me it was a strange celebration. Thousands upon thousands of peasants, poor, barefoot, daubed with colored ritual symbols and with their worldly wealth in hand, had journeyed hundreds of difficult miles to come here to feel a spiritual mantle laid upon them, giving their material possessions to the deity as an expression of their devotion to an Absolute. It was very solemn. Bleak and solemn. A wicked thought pierced the solemnity. I would be drear and subdued too, I thought, if I had just given my worldly wealth to a stained and smoky statue and been whisked from its presence after only a second's glance. Whoa, I told myself, that's unfair. Remember, the statue is merely to remind us of only part of the potential of the human spirit.

From time to time Indian journalists write about the many incredibly wealthy temples around India. They document the enormous costs needed to maintain the temples and the extraordinary income collected from the poverty of a people. The journalists suggest using the money for social causes, but British trained bureaucrats in Delhi simply say that if the money is used to feed the poor then the poor would have no further incentive to work. Indians, it seems, have been listening to American politicians.

One suggestion made by the governing board of the Tirumala temple has been to award 10 percent of its annual income to the Tirupati Medical College. If this were to happen, it would be one of the richest medical schools in the world.

The small town of Tirupati claims a number of academic institutions. Most remarkable to me is the Indian Institute of Research in Yoga and Allied Sciences. Physically, except for its size, it has a most unremarkable appearance. It is a large, three storied, very plain concrete building made in the shape of a truncated "H" and looking as if it were simply set in the middle of an old field. The entrance is just another dusty lane. Although the building is not old, its inside reminds me of antique medical buildings, and indeed, I suppose it had been modeled after exactly such buildings, the old but prestigious Oxonian structures. There are long hallways giving off to modestly sized laboratory rooms, mostly sparsely furnished and mostly unused. The research equipment looked to be quite outdated. The Institute is the brain child and darling of Dr. G. S. Melkote who is both a physician and a Member of Parliment from the state of Andra Pradesh.

Well over half the building is devoted to rooms for patients under study. As the name of the Institute indicates, the patients are subjects for research studies on the effectiveness of various yoga practices on different kinds of ills. On one visit to the Institute I watched as most of the patients participated in a group neti drill. Neti is the practice of flushing the sinuses by inhaling water through one nostril and directing its discharge through the other nostril. One staff member was studying whether neti benefited respiratory illnesses.

The most impressive exhibit, however, took place when I took my UCLA tour group to Tirupati. We were invited to watch the advanced yoga class for interested townsfolk of Tirupati. Much like our adult education courses, these classes take place after the workday. I counted some twenty students, two of whom were women and three were children. Each student had his own mat. The instructor was an extremely handsome young Indian with an almost perfectly developed body. He demonstrated the different yogic postures and led the exercises while on a raised platform in front. Literally without words, in an environment of focused but relaxed concentration, the class would assume a posture, hold it while directing awareness to the parts of the self involved, then respond to the instructor to go on to a new posture. Some postures were difficult and a few of the youngsters could not keep up. The instructor moved with fluid grace, lithe but disciplined, teacher and helper, and the class responded with devout attention and absolute obedience. It was an incredible scene.

As my UCLA tour group watched the yoga class, I heard one of the more chic and affluent members comment, "The only authentic yoga is taught by our swami in Beverly Hills." And she meant it.

The Spirit of Tirupati

My first visit to Tirupati and the Institute had come about as a sequel to the Ananda Marg experience in Madras. One near victim of the terrorists' recruiting during that episode was my young friend Abhijit and another was a young man named Nandagopal. Both young men had applied for graduate school scholarships in England but Nandagopal was ill the day of the interview and it was Abhijit who went to England and earned his Ph.D. there.

Nandagopal was left behind when the bioengineering department at the Indian Institute of Technology, Madras, lost its leader with the escape of its chief, and Nandagopal was cast loose. It was especially difficult for him because he had been orphaned early in life (he told me, but an Indian friend disputes this). It appears, however, that he was adequately provided for by a financial legacy. He was terribly lonesome and at wits' end at missing his chance for advanced schooling. He did, however, have a sponsor, the same Dr. Melkote of the Yoga Institute and it was Dr. Melkote who made a place for Nandagopal in Tirupati.

A year after the Ananda Marga episode at the IIT, Madras, I wrote to the remaining members of the bioengineering department that I was returning to India and would like to meet with them. By then the department was pretty well dispersed and Abhijit had left for England. I discovered that Dr. Srinivasin, who was the chief research expert, was on a sabbatical and that Nandagopal had moved to Tirupati. When Nandagopal discovered I could not come to Tirupati, he sent me several urgent letters to tell me that he would arrange to meet me in Hyderabad in east-central India where I was going to experience the centuries old Muslim culture of the great Nawobs (Nabobs) and visit the riches of the Salar Jung Museum.

The meeting with Nandagopal tore deeply at my heart-strings. Being unable to afford the trip himself, he had appealed to Dr. Melkote to come. So here was the 78-year-old good doctor and M.P. and the 19-year-old orphan coming all the way from Tirupati to Hyderabad to see me. Nandagopal came into my room shyly and held out a package in gift wrapping. He said it was a present to me and would I please open it. I unwrapped it carefully to find a slender box filled with small items, each wrapped separately in still a different gift wrap paper. I undid the small packages. They were: a small scratch pad, a lead pencil, a twist of ribbon, a hand printed poem, and a gaily printed card that read "I LOVE YOU". Ever after I thought of this as my love package. Such charm, such ingenuousness, such love. And although Nandagopal went on to study in Australia and won his Ph.D. there and I have not seen him in years, I will never forget the love and trust he showed me that day in Hyderabad. And I am grateful, too, that Dr. Melkote was kind and understanding enough to bring him.

Dr. Melkote also later took in, temporarily, on the staff, Dr. Srinivasin, from the IIT. With such talent coming to Tirupati, it seemed that the Institute would be in contention as the premier biomedical/yoga research institution in all India.

Academia in India, however, as in the U.S., operates via academic politics. The All-India Institute in Delhi is reputed to possess the best medical research facility in India while Tirupati is still relatively unknown. Yet the large University hospital in Delhi is doubtless the most unkempt, filthiest, most unattended hospital unit I have ever seen and the medical school itself is a model of the most unused, pretentious, dusty relic I hope never to see again. On the other hand, the Institute in Tirupati is sparkling clean, the staff busy and productive, and the patients well cared for.

It was most fortuitous that as I was planning the UCLA Extension tour of India, I learned that a hotel rest-house had just been built in Tirupati and so I would be able to take the group there. The hotel, in fact, had been given two stars.

Hotel Oorvasi turned out to be an outstanding example of India's trying to catch up to the 20th century. Our group was among its first guests and we experienced the pains of a commercial transformation. The hotel was, then, sort of a combination of the traditional Indian government rest-house (really bare bones for travellers) and a modern hotel. The rooms were very large, beautifully light and clean and with giant windows opened to the outside. Each room also had an anteroom with chairs and coffee table for chatting and an outside call-bell system. In the bedrooms there were large twin beds with thick foam mattresses, a cupboard and bench for luggage, desk and chair and bright desk lamp (light is a scare quality in Indian hotels), and there were switches everywhere for lights and ceiling fans.

The bathroom provided one tap at the basin, a new, very low (short) toilet that actually worked, and a shower with the traditional buckets for bathing. The bathroom even had a new hot water heater with its own switch!

Then the problems. No toilet paper. After the group deluged the management (two students) with screams for any kind of tissue, an hour later we learned that there was no such thing as toilet paper, tissues or even paper napkins in all of Tirupati. That's when we finally noticed there was also no bedding, not even a top sheet. Eventually we were supplied —at 1.5 rupees per sheet. Our bottled water turned out to be water still hot from boiling and cost us 3 rupees a pitcher. When you have not been exposed to the culture, it is difficult to remember that most Indian pilgrims travel with their own bedding and towels (and they can drink the local water!).

But the dining room was worth a thousand hardships of bed and bath. Refectory style, with dozens of long tables for the many groups of pilgrims, the cuisine was South Indian . . . and divine! For me there is no food like South Indian food —the paper dosai, the almond drinks, the mangos. The kitchens spewed forth bearers with steaming dishes, the great dining hall becoming a giant amphitheatre of excited dialects extolling the perfection of the food.

The exquisite food, the scrumptiously clean, light and airy rooms, the Yoga Institute, the Lord Ventakeswara Temple, the earnest service of the medical staff, the extraordinary sacrifice of the millions of pilgrims are all fused in my memory of one of the most endearing, profound symbols of man's yearning to know the inner being and tune the self to the universal consciousness. Tirupati has it all—the spirit, the love, the service, the reverence for the life of the spirit. And it is so *Indian.* It shows the panorama of Indian history, philosophy, its disciplines for the well-being of mind, and the ways to self- and God-realization.

INCREDIBLE
SRI LANKA

Sri Lanka was a fitting escape from Swami Z and near capture by the terrorist Ananda Marg. When we planned our trip, we had no way of knowing how life-saving the flight from Madras might be. Both of us had reasons for travelling to Sri Lanka. Shireen had close friends there but tight restrictions on travel by the then entrenched Communist government had made it impossible for her friends to even get to nearby India. I, of course, had been caught up in the romance and surprising novelty that Sri Lanka offered. Aside from the geographical and historical attractions, such as the Temple of the Sacred Tooth, there were also two fascinating real live people there. One was the famous physicist/science-fiction writer Arthur C. Clarke (*2001* and other book and movie marvels) and the other was Dr. Kavoor, the (then) eighty-year old physician dispeler of the magic of India's magic men.

A third remarkable, and later unbelievable, attraction moved quickly into our circle of acquaintances. Within a second of expressing interest in the religious (philosophic) history of Sri Lanka and my interest in mental health, it was all arranged for us to meet Father Matthew Peiris, a famed exorcist. He alone warrants a full story, but then so does each experience in the lands that are India and Indian-born that now bear other names. I will try to do his story justice in a few words even though other Sri Lankan adventures must share the time and space.

The stage for the Father Matthew experience was set almost the moment we set foot in Colombo, the capital of Sri Lanka. With my usual penchant for exploring remnants of days of yore, I had booked us into the fabled Hotel *Gale Face*. It had been the luxury home of visiting royalty, artists, writers and explorers. I had read that it had once been one of the grandest hotels in Asia, but a glance at the lobby quickly showed how much conditions had changed. Of course this was during the fifth year of strict Communist rule, and if anyone has ever visited a country under long communistic dominion, one knows that all former luxury is sacrificed to the erosion of time.

The hotel was a caricature. Of the once great lobby, there was now only a small registration desk. The maroon carpeting was faded and riddled with threadbare patches. There was no one around to help us to our rooms. The registering clerk said to go to the hall (about 100 feet away), take the elevator to the 3rd floor, then go toward the sea and get the next elevator to the 4th floor and walk straight back to our rooms. Not a soul was in sight. Not even the usually ubiquitous room boy.

The rooms, however, were a joy. They were, in fact, a suite, with both rooms completely open to the outside by giant concreted openings, each some five feet long and four feet high. Bevies of crows cawed and perched along the wide concrete ledges of the open spaces that were our windows. No screens, of course. The Indian Ocean lapped lazily below us. Gentle breezes refreshed our faces. We could see for miles along the coast and flowery fragrances wafted in with the breeze. Heaven!

We decided to unpack a few things, then go for Cold Coffee. We had brought some tins of coffee and tea (yes! we had heard there was a terrible shortage, even of tea in Ceylon!), some tinned biscuits, and other goodies. Each tin was large and heavy and we were glad to have them out of our luggage. Lacking space, we lined the opened windows with our precious tins and took off to get our cold drinks.

Returning to our rooms to ready ourselves to see Father Matthew, Shireen caught her breath in an inward swoosh and whispered, "Someone's taken our coffee!"

And sure enough, half our tinned gifts were gone. We searched everywhere, called the desk, found our room boy and quizzed everyone. All were puzzled. We could never suspect our room boy (who always has a room key) because room boys *never* take anything. Then the crows came back and began to peck furiously at the remaining tins. There were our thieves! Bold, brazen and cawing they pecked away. The shiny tins were a far greater attraction than were our flailing arms a distraction. How very strong they must be to lift a full pound tin of coffee. We sent a gang of room boys to sweep the grounds below, and there, scattered in the shrubbery and along the shore were all our precious tins. They were just too heavy for the crows to carry very far.

This mystery solved, we set off to the Episcopal rectory for our next adventure. Father Matthew was, to these female eyes, adorable. The rectory where we met was my vision of a real Ibsen doll house. It had small spires atop gabled roofs, tall narrow windows, the house like a grey picture of a pre-Victorian country home. The front yards, belying their city surroundings, were Lankan cousins of the English garden. It was all very British, befitting a priest of the Anglican Church. Father Matthew was, however, a native Singhalese. Swathed in a white robe, tied with a great dark, dangling cord, his slight frame reminded me of a small brown gnome. His white hair crowned his dark brown body and his body language and sparkling eyes spoke of great curiosity and a drive to partici-pate in the joys of life. Unfortunately, he ultimately indulged these instincts beyond the pale of the law.

Father Matthew was waiting in the front garden when we arrived. Having heard I was acquainted with several of Sri Lanka's best known citizens, he had arranged a royal recep-tion. We chatted a bit in the garden while he made me wel-come and sketched out what he had planned. I couldn't wait. He had arranged three extraordinary exhibits; one, his collec-tion of rare, ancient Buddhist texts; the second, a collection of Voodoo tokens; and last, the documents of his exorcism of devils in mental patients.

The entry of the rectory was a delightful reminder of those in the tiny castle clones that once dotted the English countryside. It probably looked longer than it really was, but the size was certainly ample. The length ended in a broad fireplace. In the exact center of the room, Father Matthew had put a long refectory table and had laid out his exhibits on both sides. Much like a museum tour guide, he walked me down one side, then the next, explaining each item on the table.

There were first, the Buddhist texts. They reportedly were from around the year 400 A.D., when the Mahayanan Buddhists migrated to Ceylon after their split with the Vajrayana Buddhists in Northern India. One could see the writing was the old Pali, a script not used much after 500 A.D. But the texts actually did not differ much from any wooden-paged Buddhist books still made today. Traditionally such texts are about 3 inches in height, about 10 inches in width, with wooden boards as the book covers and rough pulp paper for the pages. The writing runs from right to left, and the books are bound simply with cord or thongs. It certainly was a sight to see these ancient texts, especially for someone who loves books the way I do.

I suggested that the books would make a wonderful travelling exhibit, but Father Matthew told me that the Sri Lanka government forbids even temporary export of its antiquities. He also indicated that he was allowed possession of them only so long as he remained in Sri Lanka.

The next exhibit was a collection of Voodoo charms. Native Sri Lankans (the native Singhalese) are the most superstitious in the world. African or Haitian juju or voodoo has nothing on Sri Lankan voodoo. Chicken blood, dolls with pins in them, castor beans, and a jumble of other ordinary items are endowed with magical powers that are used mainly for bringing harm to your enemy or to heal the harm an enemy has done to you. Father Matthew recounted scores of hex illnesses and hex murders and told how this led him to explore ways to extend prayers and petitions for God's healing help. It was this interest that later led him to the use of exorcism.

It was the exhibits on the other side of the table that were beckoning me. As we moved toward the other side, Father Matthew paused dramatically. It was as if he were shifting personalities and moving into a different life. The next exhibit needs a brief introduction:

Father Matthew had become famous for his exorcisms (mind you, this was almost simultaneous with the flurry of interest excited by the book *The Exorcist*). His greatest acclaim came when he used his rites of exorcism to chase the devils from the mind of a woman who had been wildly insane for some seventeen years.

On the table were scores of photos and newspaper articles attesting to the miracle of this exorcism. Now, two years later, the woman was living a normal life in a nearby village. Father Matthew described the case in detail. The woman had been wholly out of touch with reality for all the 17 years. She had frequent tantrums, screaming and thrashing about, and although she beat her fists and lashed out, she had never been violent with anyone She did not recognize her husband or children although they faithfully attended her all those years. Then one day Father Matthew heard that a Catholic priest had exorcised devils from a tormented woman and so had cured her. He decided to investigate this sanctified ritual as a treatment for mental illness.

After all, he reasoned to himself, he was a priest of the Anglican Church (a legacy from British influence on the island), and his mission, indeed his passion, was to help and heal. He therefore prepared himself by studying the rites of exorcism and adapting the ritual to a hospital setting. I was both amused and delighted to discover that Father Matthew was creative enough to (1) use the Catholic rites in an Anglican ritual and (2) do the whole exorcism in English (so the people could understand), and be perceptive enough to ensure documentation with Polaroid photos, and (3) tape record the entire ritual.

I listened entranced to the recordings. Father Matthew would point to the Polaroid pictures he had placed in a sequence to match the recording. I was able to get a mental picture of the entire proceedings. For hours there had been a battle between the invading devils and the Father's demands for them to be gone forever. Then at last there was a horrendous guttural cry and the devils left the woman's body. Father Matthew was well pleased.

There were many other cases in which this good priest's exorcisms drove devils from the mentally ill and restored them to normal life. There were a number of newspaper clippings and other personally witnessed testimonials to confirm the Father's successes.

The *Ceylon Observer* has devoted considerable space to reports on the remarkable cures effected by Father Matthew Peiris's exorcisms. The Sunday, March 17, 1974 issue, for example, contained nearly a full page of witnessed exorcisms along with several side-bar testimonials. The following are copies of two such testimonials.

1. "I am an Anglican priest presently in charge of the Church of St. John the Evangelist, Padandura. I have been very closely

associated with Father Matthew on many an occasion when he dealt with possessed cases. I myself have done a number of Exorcisms, and of these, I would like to take two cases which may be of interest to your readers—one in the hill country, and the other in an urban area close to Colombo.

"You will, I am sure appreciate, that I do not disclose names of people or places. The two names I have used are not the names of the people concerned.

REV. EDISON.
T.L. MENDIS
Church of St. John the Evangelist, Padandura.
Vicar."

(This was followed by descriptions of four (not 2) of the vicar's exorcisms.)

2. "I am a widow for the last 21 years and wish to testify my daughter's case. She is a girl who has been suffering from fits from her infancy. As we were parishioners of St. Pauls Kynsey Road, Father Matthew Peiris heard of this case and wanted her brought to church.

"I found it very difficult to bring her to church as she used to get fits there. One day during the service as Father Peiris was consecrating the bread saying 'who in the same night that he was betrayed took bread', she had a fit and fell between the pews, but father continued with the service.

"Soon after the service, Father told us that this was a sure case of the devil as he resented the Blessed Sacrament. Then Father Matthew Peiris kept the crucifix over her and cast the devil away. Since then for the last 17 years my daughter has never had a fit nor has she taken any treatment for it. Now she is a happy working girl.

"Since then we have seen so many other cases blessed and cured by Rev. Father Matthew Peiris. I firmly believe that God has given him authority over all evil spirits, as she is a faithful servant of God. I thank the Lord for all the blessings received.

A BELIEVER"

It was an exciting day. Aloud I wished that I could, myself, witness such a cure, but it seemed that Father Matthew had pretty much cured every mentally disturbed patient on the island. What next, I thought. More than anyone could have dreamed, I was to learn later.

Father Matthew and I became friends. In particular, he wanted my help in publishing a book of his experiences. I, too, was interested in seeing his experiences told in book form, and I urged him to send me whatever he wrote and I would forward it immediately to my own publisher. Instead, Father Matthew sent me long, long letters. He sounded both timid and troubled. Whenever I went to Sri Lanka, there would be Father Matthew waiting at my hotel to welcome me. He never really did work on a book.

A few years went by.

It was some five years after we met and I was in Bombay visiting friends when an old friend greeted me with a clipping from the newspaper in Colombo.

FATHER MATTHEW PERSIS HAS BEEN CONVICTED OF THE MURDER OF HIS WIFE AND HER LOVER.

Father Matthew, it seemed, had played God once too often.

Interlude

This seems to be a good place to interrupt the strange experiences in Sri Lanka to pay a bit of homage to its most outstanding resident. Most people know Arthur C. Clarke as a wonderfully creative, solidly scientific science-fiction writer. His books *Childhood's End, 2001,* and *Journey to Rama* are particular favorites of mine. But it should be stressed over and over that it was Arthur C. Clarke's observations and analyses that made satellite communication possible. He was, after all, originally a physicist. A few years ago Indian college students presented him with his own satellite receiving dish as a token of their admiration, although India then had none of its own. He also has long been a pioneer in underseas exploration and photography. He is Sri Lanka's gem and a precious resource of the world.

Dr. Kavoor, the Anti-Magic Man

In our journeys to be with the holy men and women of India and witness their ways, it was especially appropriate that we, Shireen and I, could be granted time with Dr. Kavoor. From time to time I would read newspaper accounts of Dr. Kavoor's remarkable ability to do every bit of magic the most publicized Indian miracle men could do. The most popular and widely believed miracles (or materializations—depending upon your point of view) were the vibuthi and gold jewelry materialized by Sai Baba. It had been reported that Dr. Kavoor could do the same, perhaps even more deftly than Baba himself. Having watched Sai Baba, I was anxious to see whether anyone really could duplicate his feats.

Dr. Kavoor lived on the outskirts of Colombo, in a lovely small house surrounded by bougainvilleas of every color. The interior was surprisingly Continental. Dr. Kavoor himself was quite tall, some six feet two, I would guess, with a great shock of white hair and at 80 was handsome and vigorous.

After tea, Dr. Kavoor teased me about being scarcely able to wait for his magic show. Indeed, I was eager. After a bit of introduction and going through an elaborate routine to show there was nothing up his sleeves, or in his coat or under his tie or any close object, Dr. Kavoor waved his bare arm in the air, swung it down toward my outstretched palm and deposited there a great pile of vhibuthi. It was light grey, very fluffy (so that bits of ash and dust would have been seen upon any hand manipulation he would make), and it had come from nowhere!

He repeated the trick four or five times, each time giving us a lecture on the sleight-of-hand tricks he was convinced so many swamis use, even the most highly regarded ones. Then he let us examine his hands and pockets, and now, with shirt sleeves rolled up, he waved his hands again in the air and swooped them down to deposit a large gold pendant in my hand.

There was not a trick in any miracle man's repertoire he could not do. He had travelled India from top to bottom for some 30 years, proving over and over that the swamis' magical mysteries were tricks of the hands, not of minds or spirits. He left this world with about a 30 percent conversion rate, which is pretty good considering that so much of India is uneducated and superstitious. But I do believe he convinced the press, and that has made a difference.

DELHI'S
DADAJI

The mid-seventies were a time of extraordinary change in the global introspection that had manipulated, sometimes destroyed, and sometimes saved human minds throughout the world. Some used drugs to see an inner vision, some sought Indian gurus and some followed an austere Zen path, but in the seventies nearly everyone who experienced a different reality now began to look for ways to move back into a broader society. They sought ways to live by their new insights and to help to secure a more orderly, more peaceful, more humanely understanding world. But so many minds had been hurt so deeply by those who abused the searchers and persuaded them to drugs or to worldly rejections that enormous numbers of earnest seekers after the Ultimate Good themselves became rejected and they floundered in the no-man's land of rejection by the very society they wished to make better for mankind.

In other stories I recount meetings with Sai Baba, Mukdananda, Rajneesh and other highly visible figures who have attracted extraordinary throngs of seekers of inner peace. There are, as well, throughout India, literally hundreds of gurus, spiritual guides and mentors, either universally acclaimed or self-anointed, that minister to the lost or earnest seekers for spiritual rest. Many Western social and religious commentators malign the Indian spiritual enclaves as philosophically misguided, amoral, filthy, antisocial, ignorant, or dissolute. It matters not whether the guru or guide is charlatan or mystic. The Christian-Judaic thought that dominates social attitudes in the West rarely tries to see behind the costuming of Indian philosophy. Ecumenism is for the religious philosophies of the West and their special minions.

Nonetheless, there are one or two straightforward formulas for learning to understand the mission and value of the Indian way to achieve human fulfillment. (I refrain from referring to Hindu because religious philosophy in India is such an amalgam of concepts and paths to spiritual enlightenment.) First, buried deep within the psyche of India is the primacy of individual release and union with God. In sharp contrast, every religious precept of the West is marked by the notion of congregation. "Go to Church," as compared to "seek the spirit from within" as a primary directive, makes the difference obvious. Even the principles of social behavior are predicated in the West on the notion that behavior must be moderated because of the way it affects other people. In the Orient the philosophic admonitions are directed toward achieving unity and harmony with the universe. The West's philosophy is inextricably woven into its practical life; the East's philosophy is concerned largely with the spirit. It is difficult (and usually impossible) for us in the West to ignore the needs and opinions of "society" and envision a social culture built mainly from the overflow of individual spiritual efforts and achievements.

Dadaji of Delhi typifies the ability to achieve a Universal Good within a remarkably atavistic, scruffy, unbecoming, shoddy environment.

Shireen had told me a few tales of young men who had been victims of the chase for a magical spirit within and who had found themselves in the tiny community that surrounded the guru Dadaji. One young man, for example, had become profoundly attracted to Jewish mysticism while at the University and had travelled to Israel to study with Hasidic rabbis. In his meditations he began a quest for a spiritual guide, and after many hours of faithful devotions, a face appeared as an image in his mind. With each meditative hour the face became clearer until finally David was able to draw it in remarkable detail. He then became almost obsessed with finding the person with the face in his meditation and showed the drawing to everyone he could find.

One day a friend came to David's room with one of his friends just in from Delhi. The visitor saw the picture of David's meditation guru on the wall, went over to examine it more closely and realized that it was the face of still another friend's teacher in Delhi. The visitor returned to India, taking David's drawing, and checked with his friend. It was indeed his friend's teacher. Together they wrote to David to come.

A year later David's parents came to Delhi to take David home. They found David no longer obsessed by the need for mystical visions. He had experienced his. He had been brought, mystically, to Dadaji in Delhi. What would he do now? David said, simply, that he felt much progress in his spiritual quest and that he would leave when Dadaji sent him away. And when would that be? Dadaji replied, "Either when he is not learning more or when he has learned enough."

Naturally Shireen and I planned a visit to Delhi to talk to yogic swamis and to find the Dadaji of David's experience. Delhi, an enormous complex in the old Gangetic plain of north central India, is really two cities; Old Delhi is filled with ancient buildings that trace India's history while New Delhi, the capital of India, was born with broad avenues leading to the diplomatic corps residences and sweeping parade routes and great parks dedicated to its heroes. One might expect to find a treasury of yogis and swamis there, but much of Delhi has become so aware of modern trends that even the yoga centers seem more like the kinds of para-medical health centres that have mushroomed recently in the United States. Most of the yoga centers we visited were strictly business, albeit with a spiritual overlay.

Shireen found Dadaji and made arrangements for us to see him. I was a bit apprehensive since Dadaji was to "discourse" in the evening and I was tired from a long day and besides, I have heard a thousand discourses from a thousand swamis. I've even discoursed *to* swamis. Nonetheless, I could not resist visiting a guru who had appeared in the vision of someone Shireen knew personally.

Dadaji's small community lived in a wing of an abandoned three-storied building with a round tower atop. The entire area seemed devoid of lights. It was deserted and uninviting. The entire building looked abandoned. We managed to find the right door and entered the building. It was just as desolate as any old abandoned building you can imagine. Lots of concrete walls, dust everywhere, some broken panes of glass and assorted debris. Up a stairwell we could see a dim light. There was a freight elevator to our right and like idiots out of a mystery story, we rang the bell for the elevator. A voice from far above echoed down the stairwell. "It doesn't work," was the message. And no word of help. On our own we were.

The stairwell itself was curious. The space was wide and concreted, but to one side was a wooden stairway. Up we went, one flight, then two, then three. The stairwell opened up into the midpoint between a pair of rooms that I later realized had been partitioned by the new occupants and which probably accounted for their strange location.

We called out but no one answered. Our appointment had been for 7:00 P.M., but there seemed to be no one about. Some five minutes later a young girl in what was then orthodox hippie dress (long calico skirt, loose long cotton shirt, and a shawl) came in, arranged some pillows, and walked out. She didn't say a word. We still could not hear any noise of people around. After another ten minutes a young man appeared, pleasant and smiling. He explained that the group had been meditating in preparation for Dadaji's discourse that evening. It seemed that the group could generate energy that helped to shape Dadaji's talk.

We were offered tea, then a young man gave us a short talk about what the group did and about the procedure to be followed for the evening.

Most of the group, some nine or ten young people all from the West, were engaged in printing and distributing

pamphlets containing Dadaji's discourses. When they were
not busy with the pamphlets they worked at odd jobs to help
with expenses and they meditated.

One pamphlet covered Dadaji's life. Described as a
Doctor (Dr. Dinshah K. Mehta), his chief claim to fame was
his relationship with Mahatma Gandhi. It is said that he had
supervised two of Gandhi's renown fasts and remained his
confidant until Gandhi's death. The pamphlet also listed a
number of athletic achievements, along with fasting. At the
end of this section I am including a lengthy excerpt from the
pamphlet about Dadaji along with short excerpts from his
"discourses."

At last we could hear people moving about. I guessed
we were in a small apartment in the abandoned factory and
there were sleeping quarters in the small tower above. Two
young men and a girl appeared carrying a large tape recorder
with an old bulbous microphone and bunches of large colorful
pillows. First they prepared a cushioned throne for Dadaji,
then adjusted the tape recorder and microphone nearby. They
explained that every evening at precisely 7:30 P.M., Dadaji
would go into samadhi from which state he would discourse,
extemporaneously. The pamphlets were all faithful transcrip-
tions of these evening discourses.

A few minutes before 7:30, Dadaji entered the room.
The entire congregation, now numbering some eight people,
counting Shireen and myself, began to prostrate themselves
before Dadaji. Now I have enormous difficulty in pretending
that someone I don't know demands my total intellectual and
psychic respect, so I simply smiled. Of course my Indian
friend, Shireen, with her genetically installed understanding
of the Absolute living within everyone, had no trouble

demonstrating reverence and she was quite disturbed by my lack of proper respect.

I was glad I peeked. Marching in the short distance between the door and his throne of cushions was a perfect gnome of a man. He was short, stoutish like Santa Claus and with the Clausian white beard, swathed in a remarkably faded ocher gown and a ravelling shawl. With great dignity he seated himself, said a few words of greeting and began his preparation for samadhi. In the meantime his devotees checked the tape recorder for sound level and carefully adjusted the microphone to be precisely one inch from Dadaji's lips. One of the boys explained that when Dadaji was in samadhi and discoursing, his words could sometimes fade, so the taping had to be done very carefully. There were a few seconds of chanting and then, at exactly 7:30, Dadaji closed his eyes and began to speak. He was discoursing.

Some thirty minutes later, Dadaji roused from his semi-hypnotic state and the session was over. We all excused ourselves at about the same time. Shireen and I groped our way through the darkness down the wooden stairs and out into the balmy Delhi night. I didn't know how to tell Shireen that I couldn't understand anything Dadaji had said. Oh I had heard him all right, I simply couldn't make sense out of his discourse. I hadn't been allowed to use my own tape recorder, so I have no record to check.

From time to time I have, however, read and reread the pamphlets of Dadaji's discourses and to this day I cannot decipher their gibberish, but neither can I reconcile my Eastern and Western judgments about Dadaji's guruship. From my Western perspective I am grateful for the salvation Dadaji brought the young Westerners in their search for identity and peace, but I worry that when they resume their Western lives, the West will bring science down to rupture Dadaji's spiritual truths. Then, curiously, I become swept into an Indian consciousness and believe deeply that Dadaji's discourses do indeed lead one to realization of universal truths. Perhaps there need be no reconciliation of views.

About Dadaji, From His Pamphlet

Dr. Dinshah Kaikhushroo Mehta, affectionately called Dadaji (Elder Brother), is the Founder-Chairman of the Society of Servants of God.

Reverend Dadaji is well-known in India and abroad for having introduced and established Nature Cure as a System of Medicine and as a Way of Life in India on modern scientific lines.

Two of the three world-renowned 21-day fasts of Mahatma Gandhi were managed by Reverend Dadaji on Nature Cure lines. Mahatma Gandhi, who had wanted to live the full span of life of 120 years but was not confident of doing so, took a Course of Treatments from him in his Nature Cure Clinic and Sanatorium at Poona, in the year 1945. After that, he confidently remarked: "I shall now live for 120 years." It was only after the partition of India that Mahatma Gandhi's heart was broken (he believed his most important supporters no longer believed him).

Among the other patients who took Nature Cure Treatments under Reverend Dadaji were men and women of eminence including Sir Stafford Cripps (many names of prominent Indians and Britians were given here . . .)

*Dadaji founded the clinic in 1945 with Mahatma
Gandhi as a co-founder and trustee. The pamphlet continues . . .*
        When Reverend Dadaji was seven years of
age, it came to him from within: "The purpose of life
is perfection". This thought enabled him to build a
perfect body and then a perfect mind, both of which
have since become the instruments of his perfect soul
in the Service of God. Physical culture, muscle-con-
trol, athletics, outdoor exercises, riding, statue-pos-
ing—especially posing like the famous Greek statues
—motor cycle and motor car racing and fast touring,
hunting—specially of panthers and tigers who ter-
rorized the villagers—were among his earlier activities.
        In the year 1936, during a fast lasting for 50
days, Reverend Dadaji got definite and unmistakable spiritual experiences, which he refused to accept,
being an agnostic at that time. Then followed 17
long years of inner struggle. Ultimately, on Novem-
ber 8, 1953, the "Doubter" was converted; the
human mind surrendered to the higher Divine Mind,
and he accepted to follow strictly the Divine Guid-
ance received by him from the higher planes of consciousness . . .
        In the year 1955, The Society of Servants of
God was registered in India under the Registration
of Societies' Act XXI of 1860 to fulfill, among other
things, the following three missions entrusted to
Reverend Dadaji:
        1. To help people to realise the Divine Self
within
        2. To introduce and propagate spiritual val-
ues in all walks of material life including economics,
politics and society in general, and
        3. To bring about the unity in the diversity of
religions.
        These are certainly very different from the
kinds of truths revealed to Christians, either to the

saints or to the newly born again Christians. In this Hindu spiritual experience, God is already within. The revelation is the desire to realize that Divine Presence within.

The following excerpt is from a Discourse dated December 30, 1973 and published by the Society of the Servants of God, Satya Marg, Chanakyapuri, New Delhi 110021, India.

Creations of Different Degrees

In our series of Discourses on the subject of the Creator becoming the All-Pervading Nothing and from the Creator the creations emanating, we have seen that there have been creations that have been either oned with the Creator's Will or at least linked with the Creator's Will. As far as majority of the creations are concerned, there have also been creations—material, spirit and spiritual creations— that have fallen away from The Creator and The Creator's Will and have developed anti-will to the Creator's Will. Between these two extremes, there have been creations of different degrees, some near the anti-Creator, others near the Creator and yet others in between with varying degrees of intensity and magnitude in matter and spirit.

Creator's Will Prevails, But Ultimately

Because of the freedom of the Will which is inherent in the Creator's Will, all the creations, from the Creator unto the anti-Creator, have the freedom of consciousness as a part and parcel of the creations. Even though the Creator is Omnipotent, All-Pervading, It permits the creations to exercise that freedom of will, so long as they do not unbalance the creations and That Will must prevail against all, all that go against Its Will.

The following short excerpt is from The Discourse of October 30, 1975:

Usual Life is a Passing Phase

The Script says that in order to know what is life, do not live it. This is a contradiction in terms. Everyday from morning to night, every human being does something, thinks something and lives his or her life. But the Script says "To know life, live it not." How is this possible?

Ordinarily, people will say that if you are not living, you are dead. But what is meant here is that one should not live one's life in the way as human beings usually live. Why? Because "as it is lived, it becomes a phase". If you live the life in the usual way —getting up in the morning, doing various things throughout the day and then sleeping in the night— it becomes just a passing phase. In this type of life, behind whatever you do is either a habit or some thought. Habit, too, is a repetition of thought of the same nature. Such repeated thoughts become a part of your habits. And, such life becomes a passing phase.

Whether you live a standard type of life from morning to evening or whether you live some new manifestation of life, all the same it is a passing phase —a phase that now is, but next moment, it is gone; a phase which "now is, next moment shall cease". Take, for instance, getting up in the morning. Even as you are getting up, it is the 'now'. Next moment, it will be something else. That something else, too, shall cease. Then, there shall be something else. Next moment that also shall cease.

HANNS

The following eerie episodes began just as a long, exhausting trip was ending. Shireen and I had come to Delhi as a place where we could most conveniently begin our separate ways. Shireen's brother had just retired to Delhi after an illustrious career as India's representative to a world congress of his speciality. Knowing how close the family ties were, I naturally assumed Shireen would be anxious to spend time with her brother after his long time abroad. I suggested she would be happier staying with her brother than at the hotel with me, and so, except for a sort of ritual dinner at her brother's, we parted. Shireen's welfare was not, however, the only reason for my suggestion. In truth, I was dog-tired and longed to be alone to regenerate my energies. Despite my good intentions, I managed to offend Shireen and our relationship suffered profoundly.

In the years following, as I tried to work my way through Shireen's coolness toward me, more and more frequently an incident in Sri Lanka intruded upon my thoughts as if it were related in some way with Shireen's sudden rejection of me. The sequence of strange events made for a Jungian synchronicity event.

We had just come from Sri Lanka where Shireen and I had worked our way down the coast, sampling the coastal resorts and vendors' shops that flank every tourist area. I bought some trinkets and then discovered a magnificent fire opal I had to have at any cost. It did cost me dearly, and that night, before bed, I spread out my treasures and gloated over the beauty of the opal. Shireen commented on the trinkets but clearly avoided discussing the opal. I pressed her for a comment and finally, with much reluctance, she told me that in India it is believed that opals are bad luck. Possessing them defies nature and even being around them invites problems. Subdued, I wrapped the treasures together, put them on the nightstand between our beds, turned out the lights and went to the window to enjoy the moonrise over the sea. The room was on a slight bluff and low to the ground, so low the thatch covering the walkway just below the window reached nearly to the ground.

As we packed to leave the next morning, I unwrapped my treasures to enjoy the opal again. Incredibly, the trinkets were there but the opal was missing. For as long as I can remember I've had a love affair with the fire opal and I was shocked to the core by its apparent theft. I remember trying to reconstruct the crime to Shireen, incredulous that a thief could have entered the room so quietly and been so selective in his thievery. As I said, this incident kept coming to mind more and more often as I tried to explain the rupture in my relationship with Shireen. And time after time I would admonish myself that no one as intelligent and worldly as Shireen could ever believe I could entertain even the slightest suspicion that my friend might pinch the opal. Yet that is the impression I rejected time after time until I finally allowed the thought to remain as an alternative explanation. It was inconceivable she would believe so deeply in the opal superstition that she would blame me for buying it and inviting disaster. In that case I myself was responsible for the apparent theft. The most likely explanation, and the one most native Sri Lankans believed, is that many a vendor of gems and precious stones employs thieves to steal back particularly attractive stones, gems that are sold and resold time and time again.

To this day I do not know why Shireen so coldly and so suddenly rejected me. I do know that only her ingrained civility allowed me to chip away at her perceptions until finally I believe we are friends again. Whether my lack of diplomacy about wanting to be alone or whether the circumstances around the theft of the gem or her belief in the curse of the opal caused our friendship to crack so badly, I do not know. But the subsequent events were undeniably shaped by these influences.

Shireen and I had parted in early afternoon. I went to my hotel, the Ashoka, rested until somewhat refreshed, then decided to walk about and get some coffee. To the right of the entrance lobby runs an impressive marble corridor down to a cluster of hotel shops. At places the corridor is quite open with bright lobbies on one side and the entrances to an array of restaurants on the other. I was walking toward the newspaper kiosk and looked up from my musings to see a tall, well built man walking briskly toward me. We passed, and some twenty feet further on I was seized by the impulse to turn around. As I did, I could see the man turning. We stared at each other, then very tentatively he said, "Barbara?" and I said, "Hanns?"

It had been sixteen years since we had seen each other, not since Hanns had left Los Angeles for his home in Munich. It was an absolute miracle that we had recognized each other and it was a miracle too that we had both arrived at the one place where we could see each other unobstructedly at that one point in time.

Years before Hanns had been a visiting research fellow at UCLA in neurophysiology and radiation medicine. We had become friends for the two years he was in the States and had worked togther briefly on a research project. We had been out of touch for sixteen years!

But this was only the first episode in the saga of Hanns. Of course we were delighted to see each other. He called his wife and the three of us spent several hours reminiscing in the coffee shop. There were some quite new things about Hanns. First, this was a new wife. Ana was lovely, brilliant, and charming, a joy to Hanns after the shrewish personality of his first wife. I could see that he was profoundly in love and both Hanns and Ana assured me theirs was the love of the ages.

Four months later I received a black-bordered envelope from Munich. The announcement inside was for Ana's death and in a brief note Hanns indicated she had died in an auto accident. The implication was he was driving and blamed himself.

But there in Delhi, Hanns had another surprise for me. I had known Hanns as a hard driving cold scientist who believed only in the physical determinism of the universe. Now he announced that he and Ana were on their way to visit their Master.

It is almost impossible for a 20th century American to accept the notion that one human being can be the Master of another human being. We hear Christians calling their God "Master," but the American religious ethic frowns upon any master other than God. Yet here was my friend, a well known scientist and now also a psychiatrist, exulting in having a Master he would serve the rest of eternity. Once Hanns began talking about his Master, Ram Chandra, he could scarcely stop. He and Ana were on their way to spend a week with their Master. They were at the hotel for only this one day. I marveled at our timing!

Hanns told me a bit about Ram Chandra's philosophy and I was surprised that it was one of the simpler, more straightforward forms of yoga. Oversimplified, it was a mental technique of envisioning one's self as Knowing, and thus one could achieve. To me it resembled positive thinking.

Ram Chandra had no true ashram. Visitors and devotees were welcome to share the bleak stone stalls and gather in the guru's house for devotions and darshan, but mainly Ram Chandra offered his spiritual presence.

Hanns explained that the Master's philosophy was Sahaj Marg. I was surprised, having met a female swami who taught the same kind of yoga. I had some concern about this lady since she professed near sainthood yet was as much a part of the modern, hip world as anyone in India. I suppose what bothered me most was her excessive use of lipstick and perfume and her shiny, new Mercedes.

In any event, Sahaj Marg means the Natural Path of Realization. It was developed by the Samaranth Guru Mahatma Ram Chandraji Maharaj of Fategarh early in the 20th century, and who left the final stages of the development of the philosophy to his most trusted and devoted disciple, a young man with the same name, Ram Chandra of Shahjahanpur, in 1931. Sri Ram Chandra started his Mission in Shahjahanpur in 1945 and is the chief teacher of the Sahaj Marg (also sometimes spelled Sahag Marg).

Hanns gave me a great number of books about Sri Ram Chandra and Sahaj Marg yoga. I have studied them in great detail and must confess an inability either to define the system or grasp the practices. My best interpretation is that Sri Ram Chandra views spiritual growth as learning to know what Reality really is, and that Reality is what is going on now, appreciated without judgment or prejudice or attachment. It means that whatever is, is. One of the books notes, ". . . a human being must fly, like a bird, on two wings, one of spirituality and the other of materiality," and means that a person must not neglect either his physical and material existence nor his spiritual life. My personal difficulty with Sahag Marg Yoga comes from my notions about a philosophy of life being shaped more by philosophy and its reflective disciplines than by consideration of the impact and meaning of the *social* here and now. Sahag Marg Yoga may be tailor-made for the hectic life of present times.

A few years later I was invited to Ireland as a consultant to the Irish Medical Board, and particularly to Dr. Ivor Browne, head of the psychiatry office for Ireland. I was wholly dumbfounded when Dr. Browne informed me that his goal in

life was to go to live with his Master, Ram Chandra, and live
a life of meditation. The circle of synchrony had closed around
me. I sent each man information about the other, suspecting
they would meet. Strangely, I never heard from either again.
If both inexplicably excluded me, had my role been solely to
bring these two together in Ram Chandra's house?

The following is an excerpt taken from a small book called
My Master *written by P. Rajagopalachari about his Master, H.H. Shri Ram Chandraji Maharaj of Shahjanahanpur (Ram Chandra, my friend's guru and Master) and published by Shri Ram Chandra Mission, Shahjanahanpur, U.P. 242001, India, 1975.*

The Gift of Liberation

"The ultimate aim of sadhana under the Sahaj
Marg system of Raja Yoga is rather loosely designated as being Liberation or Realisation. These two
terms are generally used interchangeably, as if they
were synonymous, and represented the same condition or state of Being. Those closer to Master, who
have had more experience of Master's use of the
terminology of his system, appreciate that there is
not merely a difference between these two words,
but the difference is indeed a large and significant
one. Sometimes a third term is used, this being 'the
perfect human condition' or the 'condition of the
perfect human being'. Thus the goal is generally
described in these terms, the exact term used depending on the person's degree of intimacy with
Master, and his own growth and experience in this
system.
"So far as I have been able to understand this
subject, it appears to me that liberation is a lesser
order of attainment when compared to Realisation.

In Sahaj Marg terms liberation is indeed of a far
higher level than the traditional religious emancipa-
tion labelled **mukti** or **moksha**, both of which generally refer to a state of salvation from which there
is no return to the physical plane of existence. They,
however, do not preclude rebirth in higher, nonphysical realms of existence, of which Master says
there are many. So **mukti** and **moksha** are limited
in concepts, whereas the liberation of Sahaj Marg
Yoga offers a permanent release from the chain of
births and deaths.

    "There is a more significant difference. Tradi-
tional religion seems to provide, by and large, for
release only after death. This is called **videha mukti**,
that is mukti after one has vacated the body. The
Jeevan Mukta state, that is the state of release in this
life itself, while one is yet alive, is stated to be a very
high order of mukti, possible only to a very few.
Under Sahaj Marg the emphasis is on the attainment
of liberation in this life itself, here and now, while
one is living a normal life as a house-holder."

VIZAK

There are few spots on Earth where one feels suddenly transported to a different planet. To be sure, looking down upon the empty reaches of the Sinai or cruising high over the Sahara is like looking at pictures of lunar landscapes, and flying over the Tibetan Himalayas conjures up pre-ice age images of Earth, still, nothing overwhelms one with the feeling of otherworldliness like the lands of mid-east coastal India.

In the days when sea captains explored every coast and land for new commerce, when conquests for Church and King occupied every inlet and isle and the East India Company began its rule of India, the two long coasts of India were dotted with tiny colonies that pledged their separate allegiances to France, England, Spain and Portugal.

Organized commercialism, however, was not long in coming. The Dutch came first in 1595, followed by the British in 1600. The French did not probe Indian resources until

1665 and did not establish a permanent settlement until they settled in Pondicherry in 1720 where an enclave still exists. Vasco da Gama led the Portuguese to the Malabar coast (southwest India) in 1497 and established their colony, Goa, in 1510. And while they seized their share of the spice trade, their chief emphasis was on controlling the seas. The Portuguese became known for their cruel and ruthless tactics and except for Goa they had little impact on Indian life.

Bit by bit, piece by piece, province by province, the British combined commerce and industry, politics and war to gain dominion over India. The great, flamboyant Moghul empire, along with its liaisons with Hindu rulers, was collapsing and native Indian rule once more fell back to local stewardship. The tiny enclaves of a dozen European origins lost their markets to new patterns and techniques of commerce and dwindled into disuse and decay. Today much of Southern India remains almost unchanged from the seventeenth century.

Not too long ago, the growing pains of India's socialism made travel around the subcontinent difficult. There were, however, some advantages. With virtually no planes in the sky except the State-run Indian Airlines, pilots were free to use air space pretty much as they pleased and often this afforded us curious adventurers some extraordinary views of the landscapes below. One especially accommodating pilot was at the helm when I first flew into Vizakapatnam (Viza-kah-paht-nam, often shortened to Vizak or Vizag).

The spectacle below was truly unearthly. Scattered about, as if placed by some master geometer, were small hills in shapes of cones and triangles and bubbles, all set in place on an utterly flat surface that gleamed venetian red. Far off in the distance to the west, I could see soft green rolling hills spilling down from the Eastern Ghats (mountains), the kind of landscape we are familiar with. But here, along the coast, were verdant fields of pineapple, mango orchards, great green-glowing fields of grain, against an earthy background that was ten-fold a brighter red than the red clay of Georgia back home. And, as if to emphasize the strangeness of the contrasting colors, here and there were the geometrically shaped hills. It is a bizarre landscape.

The scene became even more dramatic as the ocean came into view. Incredibly blue, the waters of the Bay of Bengal washed softly against the red-stained sands of Vizak. The stark eerieness was underscored by the lack of traffic on the roads. One could see only an occasional cart and driver and one or two tiny tractors. The town itself was spread out over many miles. No crowding here! I looked for the University and could spot only a few buildings I thought might be it, and later discovered that each building literally had its own acreage and fields. Actually, it looked quite desolate for a major university.

My friend, Ram Rao (Ram is short for Ramakrishna), met me at the airport. Tall, solidly built and incredibly handsome for a University professor, he was the reason for my visit. He had created a unique department that investigated, almost exclusively, paranormal phenomena, but more about that in a moment.

Ram took me in a taxi to the University Guest House (few professionals, and especially few educators, can afford automobiles; taxis are for the convenience of guests). The campus was, indeed, desolate. Most students and faculty were off on a holiday, and with so few people about, the distances between campus buildings seemed enormous. As at the Indian Institute of Technology in Madras, the University grounds were kept pretty much in the natural state with brush straggling everywhere, and little paving of the campus roads.

The Guest House was a bit like old British gate cottages on estate grounds except that the cottage was in a state of rather serious disrepair. Paint peeled, boards were missing from porch and stairs, no glass or screens were in the windows, and the bathroom was crusty with rust. There was, however, a delightful house boy whose job it was to cook meals and keep the place clean. I watched as a huge bug flew in, but was assured the great ceiling fan would keep most invading insects circulating. Ram made a date for dinner then cautioned me against walking about across the fields. Seems a student was killed by a cobra just the week before. It was even more unsettling to learn that I was not staying in the Raos' guest cottage because Ram's wife had had a scary encounter with a king cobra just a few days earlier.

The view from the guest house was spectacular. From my cot in the bedroom, gratefully shielded from insects by the mosquito netting, I could see our shallow hill dip gracefully into the sparkling now indigo sea, the red soil and grey-tan brush looking every bit like a Van Gogh painting, a broad speckled scene broken only by an isolated stone cottage with grey thatched roof. The stillness was remarkable. Occasionally one could hear the crunch of gravel as an ox-cart passed by on the nearby road; otherwise all was still with only the leaves rustling and the waves lapping.

Ram Rao, with a Ph.D from the United States, headed a unique University department. He was head of the Department of Psychology and Parapsychology. While Westerners might think it natural for the first ever official department of parapsychology to be in India, traditionally India has been much more conservative than the West in recognizing adventures into the unorthodox areas of science. Indian academia has conquered enormous obstacles in its pursuit of scientific recognition and it is particularly timid about authorizing any deviations from the scientific straight and narrow. Nonetheless, Dr. Rao had sweated, researched, and politicked his way to an eminent position at the University and had managed to gain recognition for his first love, psychical research. He deserved the honor, for in addition to hard work and vision, he was an excellent scientist and researcher.

For our early supper, Ram had gathered two of his research assistants and a visiting scientist from the West Indies. Aside from the food and the way it was eaten, it could have been any social gathering of academics with similar interests at home. There were at least six different kinds of casserole dishes, some sliced tomatoes and a bowl of yogurt. The problem for me was the total absence of silverware. I watched the other diners for the entire meal trying to discover how they could eat the watery yogurt with just their hands. The entire bowl of yogurt disappeared magically. I never did discover the trick, but I did wonder how my friend Ram could move so easily between his Indian home life and the Western academic world he so yearned to join, moving from eating with tools to eating with the hands. Privately, I was delighted that there were no attempts to explain the local customs.

After dinner was a time for research tales. The West Indian was completing a Ph.D. project and had marvelous descriptions of the Indian psychics he had been studying. One incident in particular fascinated him. It seems a nearby ascetic was widely known for his ability to teleport himself to the outer limits of the galaxy. This particular yogi would seal himself in a meditation hut for days at a time while he prepared himself for his galactic travels. Outside the hut would be placed a bowl of porridge and a bowl of milk with two devotees to guard the food so that it could be used only by galactic beings. Midway during the swami's isolation the porridge and milk would suddenly disappear. When the ascetic's hut was opened after a period of time, he would be found in a trance, holding wisps of fresh flowers in his hand. He would then report that he had been to the sun and moon, visited planets that had welcomed him and showered him with flowers. He returned to Earth by sliding down the Milky Way. The entire ashram was devoted to this guru of the galaxies.

I visited Vizak several times until Dr. Rao finally left for a position in the U.S. Each time I learned more and more about the inner spirit of India mainly because the people there accepted me as a colleague and not as a traveller there only to observe. And because my Indian experiences have been so consistently ones of participation in Indian life, I cannot merely report impressions or statistics to describe the spirit of India. Instead, I can best convey the remarkable nature of India by giving you my loving preceptions. On one occasion, for example, I was caught in Vizak in the middle of one of India's famous strikes.

Just before I was to leave for Vizakapatnam, I was advised that an imminent general transportation strike would bring all travel to a complete stop in Andra Pradesh and could easily last for weeks. There are a few states in India where violence and rebellion and terrorism lie always just below the surface and Andra Pradesh, the state of Vizak, is one of them. Since the activities of Ram's department at the University were important to my research, I determined to risk the trip regardless of hazards. Incidentally, the University was sometimes referred to as Waltair University and as Andra Uiversity at other times. I really never did figure out the true name of the University. I suspect the ambivalence is simply a reflection of the Indian ability to see one as many and many as one.

Again Ram met me at the small airport, this time, however, in a private car, the car of a union official designated as an official vehicle for the duration of the strike. All transportation except that authorized by the Transportation Union was prohibited. No trains were permitted to run and no private automobiles were allowed on the road. Vizak's quiet intensified into a nightmarish silence. At the University Ram walked me to his science building, and while we and a few graduate students were having a seminar, I could hear voices outside getting louder and louder. We rushed to the windows and could see a crowd of students heading toward us. Then, just below where we were on the second story, they began to gather and look up at us. Ram warned us against speaking out at all. The students told us to walk home promptly and not to go out again until the strike was settled. Otherwise our safety could not be guaranteed. They had already burned all the cars in sight and were starting on the motorbikes. I was struck by their controlled actions. True, they were being destructive, but the destruction was confined to very specific things, namely, elements of transportation. True, all the strikers carried clubs of some kind and they were angry, but they also were disciplined in their acts of defiance. Somehow it all made sense. Not that all or even most strikes in India are so controlled, but transportation strikes have evolved a certain tradition—noise, refusal to work, of course, and *directed* violence, that is, directed toward specific elements related to the strike action.

Since that time I have encountered many serious strikes in India and have been hung out to dry several times by transportation strikes. But the general strike that made my heart bleed for India was the incredible school strike in 1978. It was sad enough to read about the violence around the colleges and universities, but the real devastation of the strike was brought home to me profoundly on one visit to Ram and Vizakapatnam. During a family reunion lunch on the Raos' patio, his two daughters could no longer contain their agony. There had been no school for some seven months and with the school term nearly over, both girls would lose an entire year of schooling. University students in far-off Delhi, striking for more student privileges, had been able to end all school activities throughout India. And in typical Indian fashion, everyone talked but no one took action. Time is forever in India; people are always. It was not, in fact, until Indira consolidated her power and decreed an end to strikes that strikes came under enough control to save India from fatal errors of political power struggles.

I have also pondered long over another seeming contradiction. On one visit to Vizak Ram took me on a drive inland to a famous Hindu temple, this one dedicated to Ganesh. It was situated traditionally, that is, built atop the tallest hill in the region. Pilgrims walked the ten winding miles to the top as tokens of devotion to the deities, but Ram and I drove to near the top before we started our walk. Also in accord with long tradition, the streets below the temple were lined by tiny shelters and counters displaying religious trinkets, pigments for painting holy signs on the face, and tin or paper images of deities. At the level of the temple here, as is usual, the long walk to the entrance is lined with officially recognized stalls selling religious wares. These selling stalls near the temple proper are generally well kept, as is the broad walkway into the temple.

The temple is enormous, one side studded from top to bottom with carvings of various deities, and several walkways lined with statues of deities nested like a maze within each other until one comes to the inner sanctum itself. Only professed Hindus are allowed within the inner sanctum, and I was suddenly seized by distress and sadness as Ram excused himself to enter alone.

Here I was, a respecter of individual beliefs, a longtime student of Indian philosophies, truly neutral in opinion, and deeply desiring to understand my fellow man, and here at the climax of the temple visit, I was denied the experience of the deity's shrine. I had never felt discrimination so keenly. But yet another shock impression stole my mind's attention. I realized, with a profound awe, that my friend, who was at home in the West and whose future lay in the West, that this friend was paying his respects to a deity that had the head of an elephant. Worse, the very second this thought crystallized in my mind, I recoiled with distaste for myself and the insular education and discipline in social arrogance that made me recognize the difference.

I took the UCLA Extension tour group to Vizak. One of the students whom I had met on other trips told me she had a special treat for me, but that I must come alone with her. My tour group was in good hands. I could escape for an hour or so. We walked a few miles to a temple by the sea. As usual it was situated on a rise and was surrounded by carvings and statues. I watched worshipers paying their respects to the different deities and stopping to give a flower and light a candle to the main deity of the temple. An enormous, brightly colored rug was spread in front. To one side a young father was teaching his son the chants and prayers to the deity.

My guide took me toward the back and on up to the highest level of the temple. There, in a shrine set aside by itself, was a gloriously sculpted deity, bouquets placed all around and flowers strewn in front, candle flames flickering even in broad daylight, and some ten members of a family chanting in prayer in front of the deity. I realized that the entire group was dressed in the elegant gold finery reserved for weddings.

A special ceremony was taking place. My student guide explained that this family had prayed to this particular deity for special favors to recover from a misfortune. They had been marvelously blessed and were giving a ceremony to the deity in thanks for the help. The ceremony was a wedding of the deity to a female deity. As a three-piece band played in the background, the priest performed an elaborate wedding ritual with the family participating as the proper family of the deity. It was a joyful event and perhaps much the same as it was 5000 years ago. I was caught in a time warp and was, in a sense, loath to leave this living drama of such long-ago visions of the relationships between men and gods.

THE OTHERS:
PART I

Rajneesh

The people of India make it difficult for even the most serious student of their culture to arrive at meaningful conclusions. To the Western ear, Indian discussions of ways of life seem always to contain an echo of what we now call "being defensive," a most unwarranted interpretation. Indian concepts about life and its meanings embody two principles quite foreign to Westerners: a broad tolerance for the beliefs of others and a vision of Reality in which all life possesses equal potentiality rather than being composed of a heaven and a higher authority. At the same time there is, throughout India, a universal desire to be understood but much of India lacks the special, modern communications skills to help the Westerner understand her.

There are, for example, a thousand gems of philosophic insights into the meaning of life by all manner of Indians, but to the Western analyst, the reasons for the beliefs are jumbles of story and fantasy with only occasional facts. For the non-analytic or casual visitor to India, this can have considerable romantic appeal and gain a convert, or it can cause disgust and rejection of Hindu philosophy.

The problem for the teacher or experienced friend is how to refrain from offering advice on the validity of one or another bits of yoga or meditation or other Hindu philosophy.

Take Rajneesh, for example. I first met Rajneesh the night he and his followers were celebrating their leaving Bombay. The city had received thousands of complaints about the rowdiness, drug use and free sex going on in Rajneesh's headquarters and had ordered him out of Bombay. The leave-taking celebration was held in an apartment where some 50 or 60 orange-clad devotees, all Westerners, danced free-style (one local journalist reported it as disco dancing), hands and feet pumping away in place, great grins on their faces, and much long, dirty hair flying around their dye-stained, decorated bodies. The sounds were mixtures of singing and chanting with everyone having one hell of a good time. I suspected most of the crowd was high on hashish. At one end of the living room was Rajneesh, doling out blessings and sweets.

Rajneesh and followers moved to Poona, about 120 miles southeast of Bombay, a town long known for serious religious devotions and for nearby Lonavla, the home of the Yoga Research Institute, a tiny, somewhat lethargic institute begun when a UCLA psychophysiologist left his research equipment there.

Rajneesh learned some incredibly modern entre-
preneurisms in Bombay. First, he made his new headquarters
invasion-proof, ensuring that no one could get a first-hand
observation of activities in the ashram, whether drug use,
excessive free sex, or other unorthodox practices, and he in-
stituted high level PR. No guru or swami ever received as
much Indian and world-wide press as Rajneesh.

Above all things, Rajneesh is (was) extremely bright.
He began life both as a scholar and a seeker of spiritual truths.
He reports his first experience with samadhi came at age
seven, and full Enlightenment at twenty-one. He became a
professor of philosophy and claims extensive training during
previous incarnations in all religious practices known in India,
including Sufism, Tao, Buddhism, and Christianity. He also
reports having studied Tantric Hinduism, which either accounts for his heavy emphasis on sex as a devotional practice
or is the perfect excuse for it. He wrote a series of articles on
"Tantric Sex" for *The Illustrated Weekly of India* in 1977, and
these reveal not only detailed knowledge about Tantric rituals
and meanings of sex as an aid to spiritual fulfillment, but he
discusses at length the need for good sex for modern psychological fitness. His knowledge of the psychology of sex is as
good as Dr. Ruth's, but he is a much more vocal advocate of
regular practice.

Rajneesh's books and philosophic teachings are really
excellent presentations of much standard Hindu philosophy
and are convincing scholarship for many a well-schooled
Westerner. At the same time, particularly in lectures, he adds
spice to his special creed for living by such things as an hour's
humorous critique of the colloquialism for the sex act that

begins with "F," beginning with the statement that it is the most beautiful word he ever heard. This mix of the serious and erudite with vulgarity and hash-heightened rituals makes it difficult not to condem Rajneesh as charlatan or plain pornographer or crook, even in India where tolerance usually has priority over unfavorable judgment.

Being fairly knowledgeable about Hindu beliefs and practices and about self-proclaimed godmen, I have two problems in discussing Rajneesh. First, I cannot, intellectually or emotionally, recognize his claim to the titles of Bhagwan or Sri, the first meaning God and the second meaning honored one, honored sir, or sometimes, saint. I am always distressed by U.S. reporters who insist upon referring to Rajneesh as Bhagwan Sri Rajneesh or just "Bhagwan" as if they were afraid any failure of deference could taint his divinity and bring retribution. They never practiced their journalistic trade well enough to learn that his "divinity" was self-proclaimed.

And second, I have difficulty describing just how Rajneesh might fit into the scheme of a seeker's searching for the meaning of life. Fortunately I could not schedule a visit to Poona for the UCLA tour group, but despite this, I did lose two members to him. These were rather wealthy young women, both about 32, who had come on the tour looking for a likely guru. At every swami stop, they wanted to stay and live at the swami's ashram. Only continued coaxing dissuaded them. They loved each and every swami and at some places, such as Rishikesh and Madras—anywhere there was a swami and an ashram, they independently made new airline and hotel reservations, fully prepared to stay but always finally changing their minds at the last minute. They were also on the hunt for erotic art; I just didn't put two and two together fast enough. Two months after the tour group got home, they were off to join Rajneesh in Poona. One, very wealthy, gave him a million or two. At last report she became his secretary after the defection of Ma Sheela, Rajneesh's secretary who admitted her relationship to Rajneesh was a whole lot more sexual than spiritual.

Still, despite Rajneesh's widely heralded transgressions, few Indians will speak against him except in whispers. A guru is a guru, you know.

The Shankaracharya: Two Simultaneous Incarnations

One folktale, legend, or half-truth concerns the Shankaracharya, reincarnations of an eighth century philosopher. One can never be sure of the accuracy of such legends, still, I appear to have seen or met at least two incarnations of the same original Shankaracharya. I'm guessing that the original was the philosopher Shankar who was also known as Shankaracharya. (Acharya means a savant or learned one, particularly of a religious discipline.)

Reincarnation is not a prevalent belief in the West and many people are uncertain about the difference between incarnation and reincarnation. The British and Indians are particularly picky about their language, and defining the two words specifically sheds considerable light on why it is possible to have two incarnations of one saint appearing simultaneously. Incarnation really means any bodily manifestation of a fully realized being as well as a person held to *personify* a particular quality or idea while reincarnation means to be reborn, literally, in another body or to incarnate again. The first incarnation I met was Swami Rama.

Many people in the United States are familiar with the name Swami Rama. He first came to attention when he was a subject for Dr. Elmer Green's studies on mind-body control at the Menninger Foundation. Swami Rama is capable of many feats of mind-body control that have been scientifically validated many times. After leaving the experimental laboratory, Swami Rama began his own Institute. He had long lectured on the need to make yoga scientific and dedicated himself to this purpose creating, eventually, a large teaching, healing Institute in Honesdale, Pennsylvania. I came to know Swami Rama reasonably well and regard him as a man of great integrity and a dedicated servant to humanity. So I was surprised, when I read his official biography he gave me when he asked me to write an endorsement for his first book. He reported himself to be an incarnation of Shankaracharya, the 15th or 16th, I believe. I learned this was revealed to him during his meditations in the Himalayas, meditations he began as a young boy and continued for many years. While still in the Himalayas, he felt himself called to a mission to develop yoga as a scientific, medically acceptable discipline. He renounced his claim to incarnation and the religious duty that it entailed and left for Europe and the United States. He certainly is fulfilling his mission and hews a particularly rigid standard for the training and practices of health care professionals.

I saw the other Shankaracharya quite by accident. The Bombay ladies (of the Tirupati adventure) and I started an excursion to one of the villages near Madras (Kanchipuram) famous for its exquisite silk saris. Our guide had become ill and quite by chance we found a lovely lady willing to spend the day with us touring the outskirts of Madras. Well on our way, I began my usual inquiry about local gurus and swamis, and was delighted to learn that a local religious figure did indeed exist. This was an incarnation of the Shankaracharya, the 13th or 14th. When I noted that I already knew a Shankaracharya, I was informed that there were at least five current incarnations of the original scattered about India.

It is another piece of the puzzle about India. The deeply spiritual people who claim or are acclaimed to be incarnations of the Shankaracharya do nothing more than fulfill their spiritual aspirations, dedicating their meditations and works to God, and they are in sharp contrast to the swamis and gurus who become media events. It is curious, too, that the devotees of both the media-made swamis and the unrecognized, reclusive swamis show exactly the same degree of devotional reverence and loyalty to their gurus.

In any event, we all immediately decided to visit the incarnated Shankaracharya. It seems he lived in a small shrine about 40 miles away, deep in the Indian countryside, and was known only to local Hindus. He sat in meditation most of the day, behind a curtain. Twice a day, at precisely designated times, the curtains were drawn back so the Shankaracharya could be viewed. It was his only concession to recognition.

I was excited to be able to witness a rural, truly native religious ritual and to see a local divinity unknown to media and tourists. We arrived at the shrine somewhat ahead of schedule and watched as local bus after bus unloaded devotees. In almost complete silence the small tent by the shrine was soon filled to overflowing. When the worshipers saw my camera, they became agitated and warned me, with considerable vigor, that no picture taking was allowed.

Exactly at three o'clock, a resident devotee parted the curtains for our view of the living deity. I thrust my camera upward, clicked the shutter, and immediately felt the wrath of nearby devotees. (I got my picture despite reprimanding shoves and feeling terribly guilty about violating the sanctity of the pilgrims' devotions.)

The curtain closed again almost as soon as it was opened. Bang, that was it. You took your darshan fast. Darshan, as well as being interpreted as a blessing from a holy figure, also means there is spiritual merit in just being in the presence of a holy person.

I had at least had a glance at the holy man and I was surprised by his appearance. I had been told that his only sustenance came from devotees who brought him offerings of rice and fruits each day. Yet here was a hefty, hefty person. He must have been well over six feet tall and weighed upward of 280 pounds.

Driving away from the shrine, the car was silent. I guessed the ladies were meditating on the darshan of the holy man. Finally I attempted a conversation. A few minutes later, I asked a question that had been nagging me.

"If all the Shankaracharya gets to eat is a small daily portion of rice and some fruits, I wonder how he got to be so fat. Do you suppose he gets other meals?"

The silence was icy. My question was ignored. Only Shireen muttered something like, "My goodness!"

The Indian does not question holiness. After all, physical appearance is maya (illusion). Moreover, here was a man who had renounced the ease and pleasures of the world, here he meditated day and night almost without end. Certainly his intent was holy.

But my question came from a background that infiltrated my mind and spirit with the drive to know, the drive to reconcile incongruities, and from an inner command to understand the reality of the world. And the reality of my tradition was physical.

Here the two cultures, the two belief systems, the two value systems were sparring silently. In that brief moment I learned never to voice questions about the motives or lives of those my friends recognized as people devoted to spirituality in whatever form. They were offended by my lack of respect for the way of the spirit. I despaired that except for a miracle our worlds would remain forever separate, my friends behind their spiritual curtain and me behind my man-made screen of science.

THE OTHERS:
PART II

Perhaps It All Began Here

I noted in an earlier tale that my strange experiences in India began in her air space while flying from Katmandu to Calcutta. On the other hand, perhaps the strangest adventure of all occurred the week *before* that plane trip. The experts on psychic phenomena often warn that unexplainable events need not all occur within exactly the same time frame. I could use that bit of theory to justify including an adventure in Nepal in a book on India. Or, I can simply rely on the fact that Nepal has long been tied to the Indian psyche and history. In any event, here is my strangest time-space adventure on the Indian subcontinent.

When I arrived in Katmandu, I avoided all obviously commercial sight-seeing tours as is my custom when exploring new places, and instead hired a young native, with car, as a guide for the week. There are always risks in hiring an inexperienced guide, but there are also the benefits of unbounded enthusiasm about local history and a youthful eagerness to explore the unusual. It turned out that not only was Topgye self-taught as a guide, but this was his first solo excursion. His first chore was to find gasoline for his borrowed car.

We hit it off quite well. Topgye took me to the most interesting of the myriad historical palaces and temples around the Katmandu Valley, the seeming hundreds of local squares, and to the renowned Majum Deval temple with its scores of erotic carvings on every roof strut. I even coaxed him into taking me up to the Chinese border, but Topgye's fear of the roving power of the Chinese border guards let us get to within only about 10 miles of the border. An invasion of the Chinese was obvious. Everywhere were green road-working trucks with red stars painted on them. The Chinese had undertaken to build and modernize all main roads into Nepal and their presence was causing no concern at all here although the friendly but nonetheless military invasion was not generally known to the rest of the world. Topgye was certain they would kidnap an American if they found one near the border, so we retreated. The trip was not lost, however, for I was privileged to meet several farm families and we joined a group of women washing clothes in a rushing stream to share our picnic lunch the hotel had prepared.

All week I badgered Topgye to find some of the famed Sherpas so I could take a picture of them with the snow capped Himalayas in the background. It had become a dream of mine to capture the adventure implied by the superb mountaineering heritage of the Sherpas and the challenge of the high

Himalayan peaks. Perhaps I wanted a more vivid reminder of my Sherpa friend Tenzing Norgay's feat of guiding Sir Edmund Hillary up the grandest of the Himalayas, Mount Everest.

For the first few days Topgye simply gave me the facts. At this time of year, he said, the Sherpas were all up in the mountains, tending flocks and fields. There was not a Sherpa anywhere in Katmandu at the moment. As I insisted, Topgye became a bit irritated. He felt it was foolish to wish for something that tried to defy nature's plans. He added the argument that one could not see the Himalayan peaks from the Katmandu valley anyway. There were always too many clouds over the mountain tops. Certainly all the travel books recommend booking trips out of the Katmandu valley for viewing the Himalayas. I was luckier than most, however, for on two days running the clouds parted and I could see the mountains.

Katmandu is an ideal spot for the inveterate traveller. It is literally jammed with historical buildings, market-places, museums, gardens, and marvelous handcrafts and it enjoys almost perfect weather. At the time of my first visit, Nepal had been opened to real tourist trade for only about six years. It had not yet been over-commercialized, and I could stand and watch the famed Gurkha troops practice their precision drills without a police concern for military secrets of later years.

However much I wanted the picture of Sherpa guides with the Himalayan snow peaks in the background, I finally became reconciled to not getting it and forgot about it entirely.

A month or so later I was home sorting out the pictures of my lengthy tour around the world. I take only Kodacolor pictures so I can see the prints immediately and not have to

wait for slides. I had spent two leisurely days reliving the
scenes of each roll of film and eventually I got near the end,
to the pictures of Katmandu. They were a special joy. The air
had been crisp and clear with perfect sunshine and each picture sparkled with color. The pictures I prayed were good *were*
good, the pictures of the ritual wedding and cleansing ceremony by the river I had stumbled onto when all the tourists
were off to Tree Tops or the Chitwan National Park. The long
ritual devotions in the river, the pre-wedding ceremony with
all the guests in their best finery and decked head to toe with
gold was a once-in-a-lifetime experience. I was exclaiming to
myself over the pictures of the ceremonies and over the giant
flowers that grow in Nepal, over the quaint Nepalese farm-
houses, and the women doing laundry by the stream. And
then . . .

A picture of five young Sherpas, arms around each
other's shoulders to crowd them all into the picture, and there
in the background were the picture-postcard snow capped
peaks of the Himalayas!

How could this be? I had never seen the young Sherpas
before, there was not a single Sherpa around Katmandu at that
time of year and the camera had never left my hands, even at
night!

I am still stunned. I had the picture enlarged and gave
it a prominent place in my photo albums. But how do you
explain a picture that is but never was?

Events in Jaipur

Jaipur, the capital of the state of Rajasthan, is one of
the most exciting, alluring cities in all India. At the southern

edge of the great north desert, the state of Rajasthan has a look of great liveliness. Her people are among the most outgoing, colorful and energetic in India. Jaipur city is known as the Pink City for its delicately shaded stone and great numbers of elegant buildings. Of special interest is "The Palace of the Winds," a tall wall of exquisitely designed latticed balconies rising some five stories high all in luscious pink color. It is, however, only a facade (albeit an elegant facade), the back being a series of ramps to small porticos behind the latticed balconies. It was here in the olden days of Indian princely splendor that the ladies of the court could come to watch royal ceremonies in the streets below, unseen by peeping eyes.

Jaipur is surprisingly modern and gay having taken a great leap forward long ago, in the early 1700s, when a young ruler suddenly recognized that the mountainous terrain of the original city, named Amber, was no longer needed for defense. He decided to lay out a new city to the south, using the notion of regular blocks and broad avenues. The visitor need only take the long, sharply uphill, switch-back elephant ride up to the old Amber Palace to understand how right he was to move the city! The young ruler was also an astronomer and architect and built several observatories around India, all of which have an accuracy rivalling the most modern astrological instruments.

Jaipur stays modern despite the antiquity of its customs. One of the most remarkable characteristics of the Rajasthanis is their regard for their history and culture. Driving through the countryside one can see scores of great faded, eroding, once great buildings, many now being lived in by the poor and homeless but otherwise strictly undefiled.

You can't help but fall in love with Jaipur and its daily splash of color and laughing faces that is in such sharp contrast with the faces in Benares that almost seem to cry with the pains of hardship. Joy and happiness are indigenous to Rajasthan. The mere act of going to school, for example, is made joyful. Children of every grade of every school march down the broad avenues, sparkling in colorful British-style uniforms and singing with irresistible, contagious exuberance. The good humor of the Rajasthanis is no doubt a cultural inheritance if one were to judge from a statue in the City Palace gardens, a statue of the dog who was the faithful courier of love notes between one early ruler and his harem.

Jaipur really shines during Diwali, no pun intended. Diwali is the annual Festival of Lights, a time of celebration rooted in ancient legend and history about harvests and fertility. Diwali is celebrated differently in different parts of India, but in Jaipur the city becomes a mass of lights and flowers. Every shop, every street, every street corner is ablaze with flowers and a holiday spirit pervades the entire city. At night people swarm down brilliantly lighted streets, laughing and singing and greeting strangers with the happiness of the season, much as Westerners wish people Merry Christmas or Happy New Year.

Among the remarkable and unusual attractions of Jaipur are Swami Anandanand and his Yoga Sadhana Ashram. Swami Anandanand founded the ashram in 1961 as a medical facility to explore and use traditional yogic healing practices in the context of modern medicine. He has worked diligently all these years and has gradually developed a solid teaching and healing facility. A dozen or more local physicians cooperate with him in his research on yogic practices as well as several research physicians from the nearby University of Rajasthan Medical College.

It is my guess that Swami Anandanand is not acclaimed world wide because he is so wonderfully honest and soberly scientific. When he reports his experimental results, he reports them fully and honestly, not manipulated to significance by statistics. If, for example, he studies the effect of special yoga postures on high blood pressure and only one-half the patients are improved, he says so. If he were in a well known medical institution, such results would be heralded around the world.

And that I think is one of Swami Anandanand's problems. He does indeed attract medical people from around the world, but they return to their countries with the same cautious, conservative attitude as the Swami. At times I have encountered a dozen or more professional healers there to study.

Most Westerners would be surprised by Swami Anandanand's "hospital." It is a row of tiny, tiny thatched, reed-and-wattle cottages, the grass and earth below as floor and only a cot, tiny table and fragile chair for furniture. Patients are free to wander all over the hospital and ashram grounds. Most of the treatments are carried out in largish yoga halls, where the patients put down their mats and either practice their postures alone or follow the swami in special exercises.

Swami Anandanand is saintly in anyone's language. His extreme thinness and the deep bronze of his skin give him the appearance of a holy spirit who has truly died to the flesh and lives always near to samadhi. I'm not sure his saintly radiations helped me my first night in Jaipur or not, but I've always suspected he had a hand in it. I had checked into the Rambagh Palace Hotel but since the room wasn't ready I went directly to the ashram. I returned after dark, around seven, and was shown to my room. No one with any vision of what Palaces are supposed to be even when they are made into hotels, will ever believe it. The room had only a single window, a tiny two-feet-square opening up high near the ceiling. It had been an extremely hot day and the temperature in the room was about 100 degrees. Just walking in the room made you faint.

Naturally I stormed the registration desk. I was told first there were no more rooms, then when I refused to believe it, some rooms were suddenly liberated and I was taken to see them. They were the kind of rooms I had expected, large, clean, neat and cool. By this time I had absorbed the magnitude of the deception and was so aggrieved, I decided I would not let the rascally clerk get away with his duplicity. I refused to stay, insisting the hotel clerk get me a taxi and send me to another hotel.

Still hurt but determined to prove hotel guests should be treated honestly, I got my luggage and me into a taxi and asked the driver to take me to a new hotel I had seen on the outskirts of town. He told me it was full, but somehow I felt the hotel would take me. There really was no other choice. I was still upset when we arrived there, but as I entered and approached the desk, a pleasant voice said,

"Welcome Dr. Brown. We have a surprise for you. We heard what happened at the Rambagh Palace and we want to make it up to you. We have a beautiful suite for you." (The gossip network is faster in India than its telephone service.)

And they did. With fruit baskets and bouquets of flowers. Ever since I have loved that hotel and always stay there when I am in Jaipur. But I still wonder, do they do that for everyone who has a problem at the Rambagh Palace, or did they also know I had come to see Swami Anandanand? I've always had the feeling there was a spirit gnome riding on my shoulder, goading me into finding such splendid luxury for my stay in Jaipur. Equally as strange, however, was an event some years later when a mix-up in hotel reservations found me staying in the exquisitely furnished Maharaja's suite in the Rambagh Palace—all for the price of a single room! Apparently I was being gifted with restitution for the inconvenience of the earlier visit.

Auroville

One cannot survey the influential religious figures of India without mentioning the extraordinary philosopher Sri Aurobindo.

Known best simply as Aurobindo, he was probably the first religious philosopher of India to breathe new life into the Hindu yogic goals of life and the techniques to achieve them. Born in 1872, educated at Britain's Cambridge, Aurobindo was a political activist whose imprisonment led to his study of spirituality and the synthesis of a new system he called "integral yoga". Most students of philosophy and seekers of union with the eternal consciousness regard Aurobindo as a philosophic giant and worthy of the utmost respect.

Aurobindo's system of integral yoga does, in fact, integrate and restructure the three traditional forms of yoga (see p. 59), but it goes beyond the final Hindu goal of union with the supreme principle of life. Aurobindo envisioned the continued evolution of life into a much higher form, a "supramental consciousness" and eventually into a world community of spiritualized human beings. I, too, have created a somewhat similar synthesis of mind potential, based on my own research, going far beyond that proposed by Teilhard de Chardin, and I was both warmed and honored when the erudite Maharana of Udaipur told me he had compared one of my books almost page by page with the book *The Adventure of Consciousness* that summarizes Aurobindo's philosophy. In what may be another bit of synchrony, we had both proposed, from quite different evidence, that man could, ultimately, learn voluntary control over death.

Aurobindo's devotees established an ashram in Pondicherry in 1914 in the old French enclave on the coast of southeast India. It embodied Aurobindo's concepts for realizing universal consciousness while still in this life, and it became India's largest ashram and totally self-supporting. It farmed, fished commercially, made and sold beautiful rice papers and books and dozens of other items. The ashram became a successful commercial enterprise. It also attracted intellectuals from around the world.

One very special disciple came because she had a vision of Aurobindo as her guru. This was a beautiful young French girl, Mira Richard, quite a talented artist and writer and an excellent businesswoman as well. She organized the ashram as a business but her life's dream was to create the perfect socialists' community in which all work and spirituality was for the benefit of all. Her strength and remarkable talents soon put her in complete charge of all ashram activities. She became known as "The Mother", with total power over both ashram and city. Aurobindo died in 1950 and The Mother carried on the ashram's activities in his name. In 1968 she undertook another remarkable project. She devised the community of Auroville, a futuristic city where all could share work, love, and spiritual progress. Incredibly, The Mother somehow gained ownership of a massive acreage, perhaps 25 square miles, to dedicate to Auroville.

I have made several tours of Pondicherry and Auroville and was deeply saddened on each occasion. Except for the intellectually curious and an occasional seeker of spiritual direction, Pondicherry lies forgotten. Although my first visit was only a year after The Mother's death, the ashram was already being deserted except for a few faithful devotees and some visiting students. Nor were there signs of much active ashram life. Not even the kitchen was open where most visitors usually can find a meal. The small city of Pondicherry seemed deserted as well and smelled of neglect. Of course ordinary industry had passed her by and her small commercial fishing fleet had been disbanded. Pondicherry was not merely dying, it was dead. One could see how the ashram had ruled the city's development, and when interest in the spiritual flagged, the entire city decayed.

Auroville evokes just as much sadness, but much less compassion. Auroville began as The Mother's experiment in socialized, spiritualized community living, but somehow all has collapsed since The Mother's passing. One can only guess what brought about the demise of Pondicherry's once flourishing enterprises and spelled such profound failure for Auroville. Perhaps the iron fist of The Mother's rule corroded long before her death at the age of ninety-four. One can see corruption everywhere. Pondicherry itself has not been refreshed since Aurobindo arrived in 1914, and as for Auroville, the millions in funds for its grandiose building projects seem to have poured out as fast as they originally poured in. Here and there around the vast acreage of Auroville are ultra-modernistic buildings, most less than half-finished, with red clay seeping in from the monsoon rains of months ago. The orchards are poorly tended and the gardens are neglected. Curiously, attempts at conversation with the devotees living there, these supposedly socially aware, spiritual people, elicited no responses whatever. On each visit their behavior was enormously boorish.

Why? One major reason was political. Incredibly, the new French immigrants wanted Auroville to be French while the native Tamil Nadus were incensed by attempts to revert to a centuries-old French colonialism, especially after the fight Aurobindo had put up for Indian liberation. I gathered there had been massive financial corruption going on for years. Moreover, The Mother had insisted upon total obedience to her rule which included, strangely enough, names of her choice for newcomers, no sex unless children were needed, and other equally as dictatorial and unreasonable regulations. It is no wonder the number of devotees and seekers dwindled. Still, the events at Pondicherry are clear examples of the consequences of indiscriminate beliefs and naive trust in those who proclaim themselves to be spiritually realized.

Aurobindo, nonetheless, was a truly creative thinker. It was only after The Mother took over supervision of Aurobindo's ashram that it became overtly commercial. At the same time, The Mother became a cult figure with mystical powers.

One of my own friends, for example, claims a dream visit from The Mother who foretold an experience that came to pass the following day. The Mother's extraordinary influence and power was considerably aided by her remarkable talent for interpreting the more esoteric of Aurobindo's philosophies into language the average person could understand. Despite the obvious misrepresentations and corruption (one need only to *look* at Pondicherry and Auroville to know they have suffered gross mismanagement), most Indians, even trained journalists, will not criticize people or places once perceived as resources for spiritual development.

I regret profoundly the power-hungry nature of The Mother and her followers that brought such decay to the polish and finesse of Aurobindo's philosophic insights. They may not serve everyone's visions, but they certainly show what concern for the common good and contemplation can yield. In a way, Aurobindo's life and times may be symbols much like St. John of the Cross' Dark Night of the Soul—phases and signposts along the contemplative's long journey through the inner mind and consciousness to an understanding of the nature of life.

B.K.S. Iyengar

Stories about India's modern yogis and swamis would not be complete without a word about B.K.S. Iyengar. If you are a hatha yoga enthusiast (yoga of the physical postures), then you either have or must get a copy of Iyengar's classic *Light on Yoga*. This book contains plate after plate of actual photographs of Iyengar's yoga classes—real people with the world's best teacher of physical yoga.

When I last saw Iyengar in 1982, he was a vigorous 65, performing feats of yoga most young yoga adepts cannot do.

People who have not followed the yoga trend (and even some yoga enthusiasts) are not aware that yoga "exercises" are *not* exercises in the Western sense of repeatedly and vigorously moving and working the muscles. Yoga, especially hatha (action) yoga, consists primarily of postures, the perfection of which is to first lead to acute awareness of the muscles and muscle relationships involved, and second, to adding either movement of specific areas of the body or controlled breathing. The objective of all yoga is to become aware of the precise physical involvement and body relationships and eventually becoming aware of the power of mind to control the body. It is viewed almost exclusively as a technique for learning how to discipline the mind.

Mr. Iyengar, however, loves physical discipline. He is an absolute master of the physical control required for any kind of yoga, and he is deadly serious about his students' achieving muscle control. If they don't, he twists and turns and pummels his students' bodies until they scream. I've seen him take a flying leap and land wham! on some poor student's back, a student who couldn't quite achieve a proper yoga position. Wham! Bang! Iyengar is the epitome of physical yoga. He is, however, highly regarded for he has mastered virtually all of hatha yoga.

But of course there are doubters. As the one member of my UCLA tour group repeated what she said in Tirupati (p. 146), "The only *authentic* yoga is taught by our swami in Beverly Hills." And she meant it this time, too.

DARJEELING
ONE

In *Supermind* I recounted the incident of my counsellor in college, later psychiatrist and friend, whose beggar friend entertained us at lunch one day with stories of his teleported visits to Darjeeling. He could take his eyes and spirit self to this remote place in the Himalayas of India and return in a twinkling. In those days the name Darjeeling was magical, a place where Tibetan tribes practiced the Tantric rituals of Buddhism, and Huxley was writing about the spiritual mysteries of India. I longed to go to Darjeeling and walk in the high Himalayas and talk to maroon-robed Tibetan monks.

Then suddenly, after years of yearning wonder, a trip to Darjeeling became possible. As I look back on it now, it was a small miracle in itself, not only for what happened then but for how Darjeeling changed in such a short time and experiences such as mine are no longer possible.

For reasons known only to Indian Airlines and after weeks of waiting, I possessed a confirmed reservation from Calcutta to Bagdogra, the airport nearest to Darjeeling, but no return confirmation. I was warned not to go, but waiting longer would mean no visit at all, so I risked ruining a tight schedule and boarded the plane. It was small, a DC-7, and only about half full with some fourteen members of a tour group on their way to Darjeeling. It was in the days when India was meticulously living its socialism and aside from being given a poisonous orange drink, a soggy samosa (a small stuffed fritter) and a sick apple, there was no service at all.

Arriving at Bagdogra, there was the usual scramble to find one's luggage and a mad rush for the special permit needed to go into border areas. After pushing and shoving and getting stamped, I rushed to the Indian Airlines counter and with an unnatural display of aggressiveness, I insisted that my reservation on to Delhi was not correctly marked as O.K. status. The attendant just as brusquely insisted I had no such reservation. I argued with considerable passion, noting I was tired of mistakes by the airline, suggesting that I was a pretty important person and, all in all, doing a respectable job of acting. I was savvy enough about air travel in India to know there would be at least eight seats reserved for local officials who might have to travel at the last minute and who usually didn't. Usually I could pester an agent into giving me one of those seats. So I insisted and the airline officer resisted until I finally gave up in total frustration. I would just have to take my chances.

I became aware that the crowd at the airport had disappeared. The silence was eerie after the frantic milling around at the permit and reservation counters. Bagdogra was a tiny spot on this north Bengal plain, some ten miles from a tiny village and a long, long three hour drive up the mountain to Darjeeling. I went outside and found a young man who spoke some English. All the transport was gone, he told me. There was no way to get any place until tomorrow noon when the tourist plane came up from Calcutta.

Just then he saw an elderly man and hailed him. It turned out the older fellow had a taxi and offered to drive me in to Siliguri where, he said, I might be able to find someone to drive me up to Darjeeling. He seemed like a sweet old man so off we went, much like taking a leisurely afternoon drive through the countryside. I sucked in the lush scenes right through my pores, and dodging laden camels and elephants was like living a Kipling story. But the village of Siliguri was a vision of despair. My God, I thought, there's not a hotel to be seen, and such poverty. Looks like dacoit country, with robbers at every turn in the road.

We parked head in toward what seemed to be a local watering hole, but of course there are no bars in rural India. My taxi man shouted to a group of young men in a jeep and they drove in next to us. I had the vague impression they were hoodlums, but before I could think twice my taxi man was handing over my precious luggage where it thudded into the jeep and two of the young fellows were dragging me up and in by the armpits. It triggered the adrenalin. This, definitely, was not the way a paying passenger should be treated. Suddenly I had six arms. I twisted my body out of their grasp at the same time snaring my luggage and throwing it down to the road. I was shouting. My taxi man turned around with a look of shock. In an instant he had my luggage back in his taxi and me with it and before I could even sit properly, we had backed out into the road and were on our way.

"Oh Miss, I'm so sorry," he said, "I didn't think. Yes, they are bad people. They would have beaten you and left you by the roadside. I was so tired, I didn't think."

Wow was all I could think. *Wow.* I nearly got kidnapped and murdered. So now what do I do—hours from Darjeeling and no transportion. Hell.

My driver was tooling along quite pleasantly by now. He started to talk about what was planted in the fields and about the great tea gardens we were approaching. I began to realize we were no longer in the village but out in the country again.

"Where are you taking me?" I asked.

"Oh Miss," he said, so very calmly, "I will take you to Darjeeling myself." And that was that.

The toy train was just beginning its ascent up the mountain. As we twisted and turned around one great curve after another, so too did the toy train wind its way up, crisscrossing our path. Most everyone calls it the toy train. It is about one-third the size of an ordinary train and is complete with tiny engine, freight and passenger cars and a caboose. At every bend the engineer blows laughing blasts of the whistle. It takes five or more hours for its trip up the mountain.

In Darjeeling my first task would be to find the hotel where I had made a reservation. At the mention of the hotel my driver expressed barely concealed concern. As we talked, more and more he seemed to be suggesting I should try a different place. Oh no, I said, I'm very used to Indian hotels.

I won't mind a bit. Then, after nearly three house, here we were, at the outskirts of Darjeeling.

"Your hotel is straight ahead."

It took only a single look and we were off, hunting another hotel. Not in any part of India had I seen such a run-down, disreputable-looking hovel. My driver was right. But where to go? I didn't want to spend much money. My driver suggested the government rest house and I agreed immediately even though experience told me it wouldn't be too comfortable. At least it would be clean. I didn't know then how cold it would be.

There was no road up to the entrance, so my driver pointed where I should go, and with a grin he set down my luggage and said he would pick me up in two days time to go back to the airport in Bagdogra. There are times when I know I trust too much. Here I was, alone, in the strangest of lands, with not a person or place I had ever seen before and trusting a driver who had almost delivered me up to thieves. Yet I felt perfectly comfortable and at home.

I trudged up the brick path to the rest house. It turned out to be, surprisingly, a large, plain, concrete, three-story building. There was no one around. Walking around the halls I saw a few Tibetans lounging. Lounging? In 35 degree weather? Then I noticed that all the doors and windows were wide open and the mountain air and fog were swirling through and down the halls. I shuddered with cold. Finally a Tibetan asked me if I wanted to stay there. I registered and he showed me up to the second floor to my room. It was a pleasant surprise. It was good-sized with a large bathroom and a veranda looking out onto the Himalayan snow peaks. But it was freezing. The hotel man assured me the room would be heated soon. He pulled a heater out of a closet. It was fully eight inches square and had no fan.

Evening was coming quickly, so I dashed out for a quick walk around. The town was deserted, but at least I was able to get my bearings. Back at the rest house and hungry, I found the dining room. Every window was wide open to the cold evening mountain air. I shuddered. After awhile I was served dinner. It was, fortunately, Indian food, not grey, lumpy, acrid Tibetan food, and good spiced Indian tea (after all, it *was* Darjeeling).

There were several Tibetans at dinner but no other guests. My body heat gave out and I ran for my room. I turned on the tiny heater, and shivering even in my cozy pigskin pants, I hugged the heater. In a few minutes I began to feel some heat, but something else was edging into consciousness. I sniffed. The odor was strange, like old bacon burning. I turned around, felt the hot pigskin on my calf and saw the pigskin of my pants deeply crinkled and cooked to a grey turn.

I thanked God and all the Tibetan spirits for the hot water as the bath tub filled and steamed. It was not yet eight o'clock when I crawled under the covers, nose tipped with frost that seized me on the short trip from bath to bed. I cradled my portable radio, listened to All-India News and prayed for sleep.

Morning was clear, cold, and magnificently quiet. Blessed by a crystal clear day, I stood in still ecstasy on the veranda absorbing the deep green rings of mountains topped with virgin snows. The sun glanced off the peaks, streaking pink across the billowing clouds above. Only the penetrating cold ended my communion with the lines and shapes of nature that were too perfect to be taken in so short a time. I sought the safety of the hot bath where the sights and silence settled deep into my being. It was, I would realize later, the hand of harmony setting the stage for experiences of mind that were soon to come.

A sparse assortment of Tibetans and I breakfasted in the freezing dining room, they in perfect comfort while I shrunk in tenseness to conserve body heat. I was anxious to explore the town.

Darjeeling is built on a number of levels. The largest area, nearly at the top of the mountain, is shaped like a parallelogram with great sharp drop-offs on three sides. Here the altitude is some 8,000 feet. A short jeep ride takes you to Tiger's Hill from where you can see Mount Everest and the twin peaks of Kanchenjunga and other peaks that challenge mountain climbers when the fog lifts. And they truly are magnificent.

The main flat part of the mountain top is divided into two portions, one toward the north is a community square or plaza, with benches around the edges and a place for hiring horses to explore the mountain trails. Tilting somewhat downward, toward the south, was then a primitive commercial center. In those days the shops were very few, no more than ten and tended by shopkeepers who had not yet become converted to commercial overkill. It looked surprisingly bare, somewhat the way it might have looked in the 1880s when it was the favorite refuge of the Colonial British escaping the heat of Calcutta.

Tibetans are, of course, famous for their trading skills and they are truly sharp traders and love the barter and banter of the sell. But on this visit there were few tourists despite good weather and the townspeople apparently had better things to do than tend their shops. The best I could do was buy a few battered postcards and a single folkcraft picture (fortunately bought years before folk art, driven by tourist demand, became folk trash).

Exploring the upper level of the town had not taken long. I started back across the wide plaza toward the path to the rest house. At the far end a tall Tibetan lama sat casually on a bench. His maroon robe draped him elegantly, as if he had been sculpted there. I looked at his face and his eyes smiled. The face radiated the presence of a most incredible bliss. I was scarcely moving and suddenly felt detached, as if I were floating, except it wasn't floating. There seemed to be, in fact, no pressures of gravity, no chilly winds, no stones of pavement pressing up upon my feet. There was distance but no distance between me and the lama and time ceased to exist. The face was beatific and I was held motionless in an indefinable space, held by a magnetic pull of the lama's radiation of pure spirit.

It would be a perfect Tibetan tale if I could say that when I was released from the invisible grip of the lama that he had disappeared. But he hadn't. Instead, as I walked toward him, he rose and bowed and gave me the most beautiful whisper of a smile. I watched as he walked down the square, tall, straight, and so perfectly a part of his environment that later I was never really sure whether he did, indeed, disappear into space or whether the experience had overwhelmed my ability to see. I spent the day wandering up and down the many levels of Darjeeling, strangely warm in the memory of an experience of wholly spiritual rapport.

That was, however, not all. The following afternoon, cozy in the returned taxi and content with new explorations by cab, savoring the peaceful, solitary visit to the Tibetan temple at Ghoom and wrapped in a mutual trust around the driver and me, we began our descent from Darjeeling.

At the first level below the main town the road broke out into a wide, paved space where cars could park to see the view. Ahead to the left I could see a Tibetan temple, and then, coming straight at us, walking quickly on our side of the road, was a smallish, bent, old and wrinkled woman. Her clothes were of beggars' gray, soiled in the Tibetan tradition of rarely washing anything, clothes or body, and there was an old rag tied around her head. We were not driving fast, but suddenly all time and motion stood still. The woman's eyes met mine through the distance and suddenly there was nothing else in the world except her radiant face, wreathed in smiles, a perfect picture neither too close nor too far away and with not a single sign of personhood. It was a moment that simply was. The essence of the communion enveloped the moment into timelessness. There was no person, only a knowing of the oneness of the world and all it contained. I was transported into a moment's glimpse of infinity.

Then in the physical reality, we had passed her. Before I could ask, my driver told me the woman was a Tibetan Buddhist nun. I turned around, and there in the road behind us the nun was standing, watching us drive away. She waved at me and broke into a sunny laughter.

Like so many Westerners I have always harbored a special warm feeling for Tibet and the mystery of its Tantric Buddhism. The experience of my two days in Darjeeling was the climax of wonder about this place of mystical Buddhism, a supreme moment or peak experience, a coming together in my mind of a mystical experience created by a most curious set of circumstances. It had been, as I noted, strangely quiet, with nearly no one about. And the experiences involved the most fleeting of glances, so brief as to be impossible to create any kind of normal understanding by the intellect of the mind. Yet the feelings were to last forever. Later visits to Darjeeling were sprinkled by experiences with people, jostling among the natives in the great market or being teased by shopkeepers enjoying the buy-sell game. These two days had, indeed, been very special.

The Tibetan gods of fortune continued to smile at me. Back in Bagdogra I found that despite the arrogance of the small official and petty bureaucracy, Indian Airlines had favored me with a confirmed reservation on to Delhi.

In later years I returned to Darjeeling many times. Always there was some special event, as if the gods encouraged my visits. I met Tenzing Norgay there (Hillary's Sherpa guide on the first successful ascent of Mount Everest) and by great coincidence, Tenzing was our tour companion on a later trip to Tibet. I met an extraordinary young artist there who renounced a promising career in oil painting to work exclusively on embroidering portraits of Tibetan faces. I became friends with some Tibetan traders who searched and found for me two rare Tibetan lama medical boards used to diagnose and treat illness. And always I fancied the Windemere, a 19th century hotel, owned and operated by a British-Indian steeped in old traditions who insisted on afternoon tea for all guests and who ran the hotel in a highly regimented, Spartan way.

Tiny Tibetan maids were always scurrying about with tea and blankets and hot water bottles for the freezing guests.

On my last visit I was sad to see the extraordinary inroads a new commercialism had made. The Tibetan religious were all gone; they are not keen about the ways and intrusions of strangers, and I suspect the Tibetan refugee camp made all other Tibetans uneasy. Sir Edmund Hillary and others had created the Mountaineering Museum for Tenzing here in Darjeeling and the government had put the Tibetan refugee camp next to it. Tourists swarmed to see both, and the nearby mountain trails had become littered and it was heartbreaking to see the refugees answer an insistent, prison-like bell to line up for meals or tea or other functions. The population swollen by tourists and refugees had created a demand for local handcraft goods and the old marketplace, on a level just below the top plateau, was now enormous and busy with hawkers toting giant paper flags and rosettes. New shops were everywhere. No wonder all the lamas left.

THE LAMAS FROM
OUTER MONGOLIA

I had not really recovered from the magical experiences in Darjeeling when another strange adventure began. It
may have been, in fact, a continuation of the mystifying shift
of what I can only call time-space perception that had made the
eye contact with the lama and nun seem such timeless moments. But this time I was the pawn of the time-space distor-
tion, a puppet made to dance through airline offices, taxi cabs
and hotels until I was right with the time and space of some
more dominant psychic pull. I suppose it was the Indian equivalent of Jung's synchronicity.

The trigger perhaps was a chance conversation with a
stranger in Calcutta's Dum-Dum airport (such a precious
name!). Ranjan and Kanak made sure I was all set for my flight
to Benares and left to meet their medical obligations. A lovely
looking European with burnished red hair sat down beside me

and soon we were chatting about adventures in India. Our situations were curiously paradoxical. She was in India to document the ESP kind of psychic adventures while I seemed to be living them—at least my adventures always seemed to have some quasi- or indistinctly psychic quality to them. Each of my experiences in India was tinged with psychic overtones yet none was explicitly psychic. I am still at a loss to catalogue these hybrid happenings.

The red-headed, mid-thirtyish lady was Elishia, a field researcher for a Swiss psychic phenomena foundation (of all things!). Since I was deeply involved in mind and brain research, we had a lot in common to talk about, so much so that we made a date to meet in Delhi a few days later. Elishia was already on her way to Delhi while I, of course, was headed for Benares. We parted with a firm date to meet in Delhi.

I was returning to Benares to visit a researcher at what I humorously called good old B.H.U. which was, in fact, the prestigious Benares Hindu University, and to refresh impressions of what is often claimed to be the oldest city in the world. Situated midway between the Himalayan headwaters of the Ganges and the infinite winding fingers it ends in at Calcutta, Benares is, as most know, the holiest city in all India. It is here pilgrims from the world as well as India come to perform their bathing rituals in the sacred Ganges, seeking eternal merit for the soul. Early mornings are an incredible sight. The bathing ghats (hundreds of steps down to the waters of the Ganges) are a mass of devotees, performing religious rituals and absorbing the holiness of the sacred Ganges.

I walked again down the long, long alleyways that lead to the river, discovering more temples squeezed between the alleys and home to cows who had somehow made it through the narrow alley walkways. I watched again at the burning ghats where faithful sons performed the burning ritual for dead parents. I forced myself to dismiss my inbred stress at being so involved with death and made myself realize that death here was the ultimate liberation. Those who perform their devotions at this sacred spot on the Ganges, those who die here and those whose bodies are burned here in ritual burning are all immediately liberated from the cycle of birth and death and the reincarnations that require devotional work. I wondered, nonetheless, whether the omnipresent concern with death could be the source of despair and sorrow I saw in the eyes of the people as they went about their daily lives.

To satisfy my own needs of psyche, I spent a leisurely time at good old B.H.U. where I spoke with some of its excellent medical staff who were then researching the biochemistry of yoga. It is a lovely campus, spotted with scores of beautiful buildings, each with its own acre or two of lush fields. And to satisfy my aesthetic sense I went the rounds of the silk factories and feasted my soul on the extraordinary and beautiful brocades that have made Benares famous in still another way.

My stay in Benares (also called Varanasi), however, quickly became clouded by a sudden strike at Indian Airlines. In those days, and still today, transportation strikes can paralyze India, most transportation being state-owned. Flights to Delhi were being cut off and I was told that chances of getting out of Benares within the week were remote. The airline office decided to open only two hours a day. But I was there, each day, for the whole two hours, fussing and shouting and waving my airline tickets and naming high officials as friends. Nothing worked. There is no one more obtuse and arrogant and unapproachable than the petty local official in India. After all, it is a socialist's society and the common man is god become man and deserving of all honor.

With the airline office closed, I spent my time in intense sight-seeing and strolling adventuring, but that is, as they say, another chapter. I had a hunch my experience with Mexican airlines back home would pay off in India, and sure enough it did. Mexican and Indian airline employees, it seems, can take only so much screaming, and when you get to this threshold, you win. On the third day they told me I could catch the four o'clock flight.

Exhilarated by the victory, I was in high spirits by the time I reached Delhi and it was not until the cab driver checked in at the cab departure kiosk that it dawned on me I had no hotel reservation for this date. My itinerary had me scheduled for two days hence at the Ashoka. I figured such an enormous hotel could easily house me, so off we went, my driver and I, to the Ashoka. Deposited, I ran to the desk to register.

"Sorry," the man at the desk shook his head, "the hotel is fully booked. There's not a room to be had anywhere."

I pleaded, begged, and managed a tear or two. No room, period. I asked whether the clerk would call around and get me a room someplace else.

"I've called for other people and I must tell you that every room in Delhi is booked." The clerk droned the bad news like a funeral director. Then he stopped, looked up and said, surprisingly.

"Dr. Brown, why don't you try the Ambassador?"

It was out of the blue. I knew the Ambassador well. An old Indian hotel, it certainly wasn't in a class with the Ashoka but it was comfortable enough to be booked full too if every room in Delhi was booked. I thought it was a strange remark.

I was irritated. "I know the Ambassador. I do *not* want to stay there on this trip. I'll just try somewhere else."

Undaunted, I told my driver to take me to the Akbar, a nice, large hotel not far away. Again I dashed to the registration desk. No rooms. Then, the strange message,

"Dr. Brown, why don't you try the Ambassador?"

It was definitely raining on my parade. I had wanted a comfy hotel room with all the niceties I could think of. If these people thought I would stay at the Ambassador, they were crazy. I stomped out of the hotel, flung myself into the taxi and told the driver to take me to the Oberoi Intercontinental, an hotel I wasn't too keen about because I felt it was overly pretentious and didn't merit its self-adulation.

Same story. And,

"Dr. Brown, why don't you try the Ambassador?"

It had become a battle. I would not yield to the great hotel chains. We went to Claridge's, Maiden's, the Diplomat, and in between somewhere we stopped at the Lodhi on Rajpat Rai Marg, where my new acquaintance was staying. She was not in and there were no rooms here either. (Early on the Lodhi was a popular rest stop for hippies; later it became a very nice, inexpensive place to stay and became famed for its vegetarian restaurant.)

Everywhere the message was the same:

"Why don't you try the Ambassador?"

I gave up. It had gotten late and I was desperately tired and hungry, feeling blue and let down.

We drove down the long entry way to the Hotel Ambassador and the driver set my bags down as if he knew here was a room for me at last. I went through the familiar first lobby on to the second where the registration desk was. The clerk jumped up.

"Oh Dr. Brown, we've been expecting you. Your room is all ready."

The bearers helped me to my room and nice it was indeed. The desk sent me coffee and called for what time I wanted bed coffee in the morning. It was all too pat. In bed, relaxing after a long day, I puzzled over the apparent push the dozen strangers had given me to come to the Ambassador and how everyone at the hotel seemed to expect my coming.

I was never sure whether the events of the next few days were the "reason" or not. However I got to the Ambassador, I was truly grateful I had come.

The next morning the sun was shining brilliantly and the world seemed good again. I was anxious to get together with my new acquaintance, but decided to have breakfast downstairs in the restaurant first. That was very unusual because I almost invariably have bed coffee in my room and wait for a snack till noon. But on this day, inexplicably, I decided to go to the dining room.

I rang for the elevator and a nearby room-boy advised me the electricity was off. Par for the course, I thought. Blackouts and brownouts are everyday occurrences in many parts of India.

I went down the stairs. The last half stair circled around a tiny glass-enclosed bookshop. It was new, and unable to resist any kind of bookstore, I went in. The young manager was a delight, bubbling with love for literature and history and naturally, being Indian, for philosophy. A few minutes later I noticed he was looking over my shoulder at the stairway. I turned and saw four magnificently robed Tibetan lamas disappearing up the stairs around the turn.

I had to have them! A chat, a photo, a handshake—anything! Like so many people who thirst for knowledge, I grew up enamored with the myths and philosophy of Tibet. There are hundreds of thousands, if not millions, of us romantically thirsting to understand the mysteries of Tibetan Buddhism. And seeing the lamas, in picture-book costumes, was like seeing gold at rainbow's end and having to grasp it close before it disappears.

The young manager responded to my eager call for help in meeting the lamas. He told me they were Tibetan refugees, now living in Ulan Bator in Outer Mongolia, that northern expanse beyond the farthest Chinese border, and were on a mission to visit famous Buddhist shrines and that although they did not speak English, they were accompanied by an interpreter. He proudly volunteered to arrange a meeting for me with the interpreter.

Later in the day we did indeed meet. The interpreter turned out to be a tall (6′5″), husky Mongolian, as fair and red cheeked as the lamas were dusky yellow. He did not speak English well at all and I detected some Eastern European intonations. Then I realized that he was the KGB agent (obligatory for all communist groups travelling abroad). There are a number of English speaking Mongolians in Ulan Bator and there could be only one reason why this kind of fellow would be sent on a spiritual mission.

We struggled with communication and finally arranged a meeting with the lamas in their rooms the next afternoon. My flight time onward would make that risky but I felt it would be worth it. After all, I murmured cynically to myself, if I missed my flight, I was already at the Ambassador.

Life was swimming along beautifully. Now if I could get Elishia, the Delhi excursion would be perfect. I called the Lodhi, they found Elishia, got her to the phone (no phones in the rooms) and we arranged for a paper dosi dinner at the Lodhi that evening, and the dinner, too, was perfect. The rolled, paper-thin crepe-like dosi were nearly two feet long and were griddled expertly. I was in heaven. Elishia and I talked until late in her room. It was a good, good visit. It had, however, one disturbing consequence—I could never find Elishia again. I wrote several times and even had a friend in Switzerland try to track her down. But she was gone without a trace. I often wondered whether she too had not been part of the synchrony of the lama event. Certainly I would not have been in Delhi at this time had it not been for meeting Elishia and changing all my plans just to meet with her again.

The chat with the lamas the next day was extraordinary. Despite language difficulties, we discussed meditation, contemplation, the role of the unconscious, where man stands in relationship to the rest of the universe, man's ultimate fate, and other questions long honored in the philosophic quest.

It was nearing time for me to leave to catch my flight. I asked the interpreter if I could take a picture of the lamas. As soon as he started to speak with them, they rose in unison and marched out of the room. I was momentarily stunned.

"Did I say anything wrong?" I asked the interpreter.

"No, no. They are going to put on their ceremonial robes for the pictures."

And in a few minutes, there they were, resplendent in maroon and gold. They sat rigidly as I took their pictures. Then, when I said that, regretfully, I had to leave, they all dug deep down into their robes and brought out—their calling cards!

There is an epilogue. For the rest of my travels that particular trip, there were no more strange twists or synchronies. It was as if the meeting with the lamas had been mandated by some unknown mysterious forces in the universe. Although lamas do not usually make such pilgrimages in India and hotels are rarely *all* booked fully (except, of course, the Ambassador) and most touring visitors, such as I, do not risk changing confirmed itineraries, certainly in India, just to chat with a stranger, the whole adventure could have been the coincidence of coincidences. With time and space around me all restored to their normal order, my travels in India that year dissolved into a touristy routine. Later I was to realize just how unordinary-but-ordinary my Indian adventures always were.

SWAMI
NITYANANDA

Someone had given me the name of Swami Nityananda to look up in Delhi as a dear, sweet, enchanting alum-
nus of the Sivananda ashram in Rishikesh. When I finally
found him in Srinigar, up in the Kashmir, he was well worth
the difficulty I had tracking him down.

In the halcyon days of TM (Transcendental Meditation) and yoga in the United States, one of the most popular
Hindu swamis was, and still is, another product of the Sivananda ashram, Swami Satchidananda. A tall, well-built, sturdy
man with long, snow-white locks flowing over his shoulders,
Swamiji could be found lecturing at almost every conference
or symposium ever held on meditation, relaxation, mind over
body, or health and wellness.

He is an imposing figure. There could be no better
model of the ideal swami, the source of spiritual knowledge,

the true guru, the respected tradition of Indian thought. Yet he always has a twinkle in his eye and a smile of warmth and gentleness all the while he speaks about the spiritual self and how to be at one with the universe. Amongst the crowd of swamis and gurus popularized by the media and by media figures, Swami Satchidananda has always been held apart, as if no expert in media hype dared risk encounter with even the spirit of such a spiritually powerful man.

Gradually, over the years, as I became acquainted with more and more swamis, both in India and at home, I became aware that the most impressive, the most spiritually knowledgeable and the most saintly were nearly all from the Sivananda ashram in Rishikesh.

Apparently Swami Nityananda was no exception. Hearing that he had returned to Rishikesh for spiritual refreshment, I hired a car and driver in Delhi to go there with dual purpose—to find Swami Nityananda and to see the Sivananda ashram.

This first visit to Rishikesh was memorable because, much as with my first visit to Darjeeling (see p. 215), conditions changed afterward. As interest in yoga spread and the Maharishi's TM became popular worldwide, more seekers came, then the tourists, and the spiritual haven that once was Rishikesh dissolved into a 20th century tourist attraction and experiences like mine no longer seem possible.

On my first visit, the roads, the town, the people were all serene despite the lively buzz and babble of tradespeople all living and being as they had been for centuries. There were still camels and elephants on the road, there were still the customs stops that marked the city boundaries, and the sannyasi, and saddhus strode at will from their ashrams to the Ganges for their prayers. Even in the midst of the strident workaday bustle the town seemed almost deserted. There was an overriding, pervasive sense of calm that came, perhaps, from centuries of an all-embracing concern for spiritual fulfillment.

I was eager to find the Sivananda ashram but when my driver deposited me at its door, I wasn't at all sure about spending so much time there. The ashram looked like a crumbling deserted town of the Old West and most of the ashram buildings really are crumbling, deeply weather-stained with faded paint and are wholly unrepaired. Invited to stay the night, I peeked in a room reserved for wandering guests and made apologies for my refusal. There was no bedding, only a tiny window, no toilet and only a small basin and pitcher. Despite respect for Indian cleanliness, my conditioning to Western notions of cleanliness and comfort told my mind I could not overcome so quickly.

The office of the ashram was, however, a most pleasant place of broad screened windows, occasional fans and tables with clean cloths and bouquets of flowers on them. Moreover, the administrative assistant (most of the ashram staff were either away or in the prayer hall) was a delightful informant. He gave me the history of the ashram and a brief summary of the ashram's particular philosophy. Across the way, up the hill where the temple and communal yoga hall were, I could hear chanting, and soon my host was escorting me up the steep steps to the temple. There was, surprisingly, a large plateau surrounded by an assortment of living quarters. Cows and goats were at home here while the monkeys preferred the road below where travelers often fed them.

A few resident devotees came out to see the visitor and they were a much different breed of seeker than I have found at other ashrams. Here at the ashram of the Divine Light Society there was no rush of exuberant glee endorsing the ashram nor were there either dour looks of annoyance for being interrupted at meditation. I sensed a Tao-like attitude that let these seekers of spiritual peace feel the flow of all life, even interruptions by visitors.

When my lesson was over, I set out to walk alone around the lower ashram grounds and down the steps of the bathing ghats to the Ganges. If a scene ever revealed the harmony between nature and human temples to the spirit of the universe, it was here in the majesty of the Ganges and the temples along its shores. Here in Rishikesh the Ganges was rushing down from its mountain headwaters some miles north to spread itself across this river valley in the slate-grey waters that had spawned the legend of the Ganges being forever pure no matter what flowed into it.

The incredible silence in this vast space of river and temples and distant mountains was overpowering. I needed someone to talk to, someone to share this majestic scene with. I made my way up the narrow steps to the first landing then decided to rest a bit by the door of the deserted apothecary stall at the top of the stairs. I turned for a last look at the river and was startled to see a near-naked saddhu reciting devotions by the water's edge. Where had he come from? There were huge impassable walls at either side of the ashram's private access to the river and I certainly would have seen him if he had come down the ashram's narrow steps where I had been resting. I hesitated, stunned, and just then the saddhu turned his head toward me and smiled. He motioned for me to come to the water's edge and sit there. Then he went back to his prayers. I made an attempt at contemplation but a surge of inner joy rose up to capture my thinking mind and I became lost in a sensation of the pure joy of being. The reverie ended and I turned to my companion. He did not look especially Indian, being of quite husky build, and looking more deeply tan than the soft coffee-color of the Indian. I did not want to seem too curious, so I turned aside to put my hands in the water. It was freezing and I turned back to the saddhu to smile my embarrassment. He was gone! Just as quickly and mysteriously as he had come, he was gone.

I was unnerved and struggled vainly to analyze the saddhu's strange appearance and disappearance. Eventually I decided I must have deluded myself about my perceptions. Perhaps I had blocked out his coming and going, subconsciously wishing for some psychic event. But as I worked my way up the several levels to the road, I became more and more aware that no one was about.

My driver took me to the government rest house. It was deserted, there being few pilgrims in the coolness of late fall and we had to scour a cluster of nearby houses to find the government agent in charge. I registered and the agent gave me a key, an enormous armload of heavy wool blankets, and a towel and pointed me toward one of the small stone bungalows. I definitely was on my own. No solicitous concierge here.

Compared to the ashram's guest room, the tiny bungalow was heaven. I banged on the windows to shoo the monkeys away and unlocked the door into an immaculate room with two cots, a great Tibetan trunk in between, and a very clean Eastern style toilet and washroom. I made the bed then set off on foot to find something to eat. Here I was again, totally alone in a strange Indian place, night coming on and completely trusting in human goodness. I made my way in the early darkness to a short strand of shops that was the business district of Rishikesh and found a restaurant with surprisingly bright lights that made it look warm and friendly. And it was. I had a marvelous dinner, walked the long mile back to the rest house and collapsed in great fatigue.

The heavy Tibetan wool blankets made sleep deep and long. It was already light when I awoke. I immediately had thoughts of coffee, dressed quickly in the morning chill and dashed out the door. Whoa! I stopped short. There in the courtyard was a group of pilgrims performing yogic postures. They looked to be all European. Their leader was a tall, well-built saddhu in a brilliant crimson robe. I looked again. It was the saddhu of the ashram steps! Seeing me, he smiled and motioned for me to join the group.

How fortunate, I thought. I will have some company and can exchange thoughts about the ashram. But alas, my attempt at conversation was met with struggles to explain the visitors were pilgrims from Hungary! I watched as they finished their asanas and took off up the road to their next destination. I found it strange that a group of 20 or more pilgrims had come to the rest house in the night and I had not heard a sound.

My last visit to Rishikesh a few years later found the massive changes that befell Rishikesh. Worse, it was a visit filled with the typical misfortunes that stalked the UCLA India tour adventure. My friend Swami Rama had graciously offered his ashram for the group's use during our excursion to Rishikesh. We arrived in early evening and I was shocked to find how metropolitan the small town had become. Traffic choked the town and the roads were unfamiliar. In the confusion the bus driver had no luck in finding Swami Rama's ashram. Luckily I had made back-up reservations for the group at the government rest house, so off we went to the stone cottages. I was appalled. The cottages were all aglow, revelers were dancing and shouting, the grounds were littered and a storm of left-over hippies and assorted seekers were waiting in line for the mess hall to open. Mess hall?

It seemed the heavy tourist trade warranted serving food at the rest house so we all joined the line. It was atrocious food, served under the most unhygienic conditions. One could just see ptomaine smirking out from the food, and sure enough, five of the group soon suffered mild to severe food poisoning.

The next day we found Swami Rama's ashram easily enough in the light. It was a surprise to find people there waiting to greet us. Swami Rama had asked some devotees to serve us and several businessmen from Lucknow had driven 300 miles to make sure we were hospitably received. They had brought their cooks and all provisions and I have never ever partaken of such feasts as they prepared. For breakfast, lunch, and dinner they brought us huge platters of special dishes (all veg of course), followed by platters heaped high with fruits and cashew nuts. They even organized sightseeing and most of the group chose to visit the Sivananda ashram to take part in the chanting.

Our hosts had also seen to the laying out of bedding in the dormitory style rooms. Being the tour leader, I was favored with Swami Rama's own private bedroom. From the multi-cushioned bed on the floor I could look out through the great glass doors to the Ganges, and except for a lizard or two crawling on me during the night, the experience was very special.

My mind kept filling with a thousand scenes of Rishikesh and swamis and devotees. With one stroke of my image brush I could feel the high mountains and the tumult of the rushing Ganges, then feel the great river flow down here to the ashram in the valley below Rishikesh where it became soft and smooth and quiet. And with another thrust of the brush, I was with the sannyasi and saddus of centuries ago, flowing into a shared consciousness in this remote spot where only the spiritually driven go, and just as suddenly I would be swept into the cacophony and dust and clash of the traffic snarls of yesterday and still feel the spirit of Rishikesh our spiritual forefathers bequeathed us for our own contemplation.

I took the tour group to talk with the current head of the Sivananda ashram and I thrilled again to the accounts of sannyasi life there and to know how well the Sivananda traditions were being followed. I asked in particular about Swami Nityananda and was delighted by the response. Everyone agreed Swami Nityananda was a saint.

It took some time to track down the swami. Back in Delhi after chasing him to Rishikesh, by great fortune I learned he was in Srinigar in the Kashmir at the exact time I was leaving to go there. He was said to be teaching in a school there on the outskirts of town.

Two more miracles transpired. In Srinigar my taxi driver found the school and Swami Nityananda was there, outside in the schoolyard just then dismissing classes for recess. I hailed him and he came running, an extremely handsome man both in face and body. His soft coffee colored skin was ruddy with a flush of excitement. He knew from the yoga grapevine I was coming and he had been expecting me.

Suddenly I felt transported into a joy of the moment. The cool crisp air swirled the autumn leaves gently, melding reds and tans and lacy patterns into splendid beauty as they came to rest upon the playground's earth. The playground was large, fenced, and one could see an almost ideal blend of worn footpaths, trodden grass and a ramble of roses. Swamiji showed me the classrooms. There were three or four, all warm-sized, with children's desks and chairs and walls with blackboards. I could hear the children playing outside and I remember thinking how incredibly joyous their voices seemed.

So it came as a surprise when Swami Nityananda explained this was an experimental school to test his idea for integrating physically disabled children into the regular school system. Originally a school for the blind, now only some 30 percent of the youngsters were either blind or otherwise disabled but Swamiji taught them that everyone was special, that it was just each was special in a different way. As I watched them at play and later trooping into the classrooms, it was difficult to detect which child might be "handicapped" and who was not. I wished devoutly that U.S. school administrators could witness this extraordinary integration success.

Swamiji had more surprises. We had climbed the open stair to the second floor of this old wooden building to the rooms the staff used. Used? In each of the two large bare rooms there were long, incredibly narrow refectory tables with freshly hewn, unstained (and unsanded) benches alongside each. Swamiji called an assistant for tea and we plunged

into a long getting-acquainted session. He told me of his years
at the Sivananda ashram, first as a bramacharya (novice) then
years at Sivananda's knee and then as an archarya and finally
as a touring swami. Nearly all swamis from the Sivananda
ashram go on lengthy tours, almost always because people
everywhere urge them to come to them for a visit.

In turn I told Swamiji about my mission to India to
meet with swamis of different persuasions. It was when I indicated an interest in pinning down differences between yogic
siddhis and the "magic" of Tantric Hinduism that I sparked
the swami's interest.

"Oh," he exclaimed, "I know a tantric yogi. He can
perform amazing feats—making objects appear and disappear
—even snakes! If you like I could try to arrange a meeting for
you."

But of course! However, during the next few days the
proposed meeting itself seemed to be illusion—a bit like the
yogis always testifying to siddhis but never producing any
miracles or magic. Nityananda first could not locate the tantric
yogi, then he couldn't persuade him to perform. Finally one
day Swamiji said things were all arranged. The tantra master
had been up in the hills (the Himalayas) fasting and meditating, going through the tantra ritual of 40 days of preparation
to renew "the powers." Swamiji would bring him to the
houseboat the next afternoon at tea time (the houseboats on
Lake Dal are Srinigar's finest hotel accommodations).

At last the small water taxi arrived bearing a glowing,
laughing Swamiji with a rather curious looking fellow in tow.
He was a medium height, somewhat dirty looking Indian who
I immediately felt was Muslim, not Hindu. (Perhaps my

statistical mind had subconsciously noted the population of Srinigar as half Muslim, half Hindu, and this fellow just struck me as more Muslim than Hindu.) The tantra master spoke a little English and it quickly became clear that he simply wanted to perform and go on to better things.

The first demonstration of tantric powers was the making of water from air. The yogi chanted a bit, waved his hand in the air, took an empty glass from the table, made a fist with the waving hand, poised it over the empty glass and out squirted enough water to half fill the glass. Swamiji joyously extolled the powers of the yogi.

I, however, had seen the yogi palm a great wad of cotton then, trying to be casual, drink from a thermos. I suspected that was when he flooded the cotton with water. I was unenthusiastic. Swamiji, however, insisted on another demonstration. This time the yogi would turn the color of the water to blue. His magic was so clumsy I could see the small fountain pen in his hand, and again I failed to show proper enthusiasm for the spiritual powers of a tantra master. The poor chap scurried back into the water taxi and left.

Poor Swamiji was left to me, but because Swami Nityananda has the soul of a saint, I did not question his faith in tantra. I could never tell him I had seen the sleight-of-hand. Later I wondered whether Nityananda was only trying to please me and then, because I did not question the yogi's tricks (out of concern for the swami), he then assumed I was acknowledging the yogi's tantric powers and accepted him as authentic. Sadly, the school had been closed by my next visit to Srinigar and I lost track of Swami Nityananda.

TANTRIC YOGA
AND SEX

The time with Swami Nityananda was very different from my encounter with another famous guru then living a few miles from the school in Srinigar. Psychologists and yoga enthusiasts back home were lauding the philosophic insights of one Gopi Krishna and since I had his address in Srinigar, I set out to visit him.

By the early 70s Gopi Krishna was established as an authentic pandit of yogic philosophy when his book *Kundalini, The Evolutionary Energy in Man* (Shambala, Berkeley, 1970) came out at the height of a hippie-inspired migration to India or to any convenient yoga center. The book describes a lifetime of desire to experience the divine force of universal consciousness and it documents in detail the remarkable changes in mind states that followed his assiduous practice of kundalini yoga for 17 years and the events of mind during the ensuing two decades.

Although not universally acknowledged as such, to me kundalini is a revealing example of the way history and historical beliefs can be exalted to undeserved esteem solely by lack of authentic information. Unlike we scientists, Indians and most philosophers are loath to even hint at flaws in long-accepted religious beliefs, and so there are few documents suggesting kundalini as historically more contrived for legitimizing sexual pleasures (and currently repopularized for the same reason) than as a philosophy of life evolved through contemplation and thoughtful examination.

In the case of kundalini, ignorance about its true beliefs and practices was homegrown. From its very beginning in the latter Vedas, the rituals and philosophy of kundalini yoga were directed to be kept secret with only initiates and true believers privy to its real intentions and meanings of its practices. Imagine if you will the very natural implications of the most fundamental rule of Tantra; "The five essential elements in the worship of Sakti," the Mahanirvana Tantra states, "have been prescribed to be wine, meat, fish, parched grain, and the union of man and woman." For seekers of spiritual fulfillment the symbolism of the first four as holy sacraments may have seemed obscure but practice of the sex act as a way to express devotion to the divine spirit must have been a welcome release for inborn passions. It is easy to understand how cult outsiders could create scores of fanciful myths from the bits and pieces of secret tantra religious practices they may have been able to snoop out.

Two thousand years later I, too, heard the rumors! I remember asking the librarian at the Vedanta Study Centre for books on Tantra (Hindu, not Buddhist tantra) and he gave me a smile and a short lecture on being careful to discriminate between considered historical reports and myth. Now, after sifting through a great deal of Tantric and Hindu literature, I think I understand the place of Tantra in Indian philosophy both long ago and now.

Some interpreters have come to believe, as I do, that the sexual emphasis in tantric Hinduism originated as simply one way to cope with the place of sex in communities. Most cultures have reserved the role of sexual activity exclusively for procreation and subject to God's Will and the way the prophets interpret God's Will. All such cultures, especially in the Christian era, were then also obliged to build codes of conduct to ensure that sexual activity served God's purpose, not man's pleasure. Tantra developed the opposite approach. The sages decreed the union of man and woman to be a religious sacrament and a way to achieve union with the divine consciousness. As with yoga in general, however, tantric yoga relies primarily on traditional mind-body disciplines to achieve spiritual realization.

As a result, tantric philosophy is heavily involved with the experience of states of consciousness accompanying biological changes during yogic practice and spiritual devotions. It was Tantra that elaborated the philosophy of the divine power (Sakti; Shakti) that exists within everyone and is, in fact, asleep "coiled away like a sleeping serpent (kundalini) at the root of the spine." Then through the practice of the asanas (yogic postures), pranayama (controlled breathing), and the saying of the mantra, the spiritual channels of the body are cleared. As the kundalini rises within, it excites special centers (lotuses; chakras) at different levels of the body and at different levels of spiritual achievement, each state identified by changes in biological function and perception. Finally, at the highest level, the spirit joins with the divine spirit.

There are a number of fascinating conjectures about Tantric Hinduism that easily come to mind. I suppose the first and most obvious is comparing the sensations of orgasm with the sensations reported for the experience of the rising inner fire of kundalini (or samadhi). It doesn't take a whole lot of reading between the lines to become convinced that the mind and body sensations of the two are amazingly similar, if not identical. However, with no authoritative reference to confirm this conclusion, it is difficult for Westerners to understand how normal sexual behavior can be masqueraded as a religious devotional practice for more than 2000 years. On the other hand, it is the Westerners who buy Pet Rocks and Mood Rings.

Anthropologists do suggest that Tantra developed as a practical technique for dealing with sex behavior within social groups, and the sacred injunction for complete secrecy about its rituals and practices let Tantra flower in the traditional Indian environment of religious tolerance. Other benefits of tantric yoga were also claimed over the centuries: the ecstasy of samadhi and the realization of occult powers. Both of the latter, of course, are shared with the mainstream of Hindu philosophy. I suspect, however, that the revived interest in Tantra during the 1970s stemmed from the myths about its sanction of sexual adventures. Certainly Rajneesh (see p. 192) allowed active reference to tantric philosophy in the practices recommended in his ashrams.

Now I was about to meet the new prophet of kundalini yoga. The only other modern authoritative work on kundalini was Arthur Avalon's (Sir John Woodroffe) book *The Serpent Power* first published in 1919. This scholarly work emphasizes the philosophy of the yogic practices of postures and breath control in kundalini yoga and claims the author was *never* told of any sexual overtones to tantric devotions during decades of research on Tantra. Perhaps the author doth protest too much!

In contrast, the wonderful part of Gopi Krishna's book is his detailed unburdening of both the negative and positive effects of his 17 years of yogic practice and subsequently altered mind states. The exasperating part of the book is that although the awakening of the kundalini and the physical sensations as the serpent's fire rises through the body and involves each chakra are thoroughly described, sex is never once mentioned.

Gopi Krishna's book, nonetheless, makes an important contribution to the understanding of the human mind. He painstakingly analyzes kundalini in terms of the Jungian psyche and modern notions about states of awareness and provides considerable insight into the role of mind and consciousness in spiritual experiences. Of course Jung's concepts are rooted in yogic philosophy.

My driver found the Pandit's home without difficulty and I was surprised to see a large, substantial single residence. After enquiring for Gopi Krishna at the door, within a few minutes a young girl showed me upstairs to the yoga master. He was in a small room, quite a large man sitting on the floor with one leg bent under him. He had a Kashmiri shawl around his shoulders and was surrounded by massive volumes of books scattered about on the floor. The Pandit was somewhat annoyed by my impromptu visit although he did remember I had written to him. I asked a few of the usual questions one always asks a yogi but he was much more interested in talking about the books that had been brought to him by a devotee from Delhi. He flipped through them restlessly and began sermonizing on how the ancient philosophies of India could be useful in solving the world's problems if people would only listen. It was not long before he launched into a biting criticism of the behavior of American youth. He could deal with it, he insisted.

The strategy was clear. It was nearly always the same, only the swami changed. Each believed world understanding would improve if the world, and especially the United States, could hear his message, and each requested help to come to the U.S.

The great swami migration of the 70s was said by many to have its roots in the prophetic Hindu concept of world-cycles. Most swamis deeply believe that the long era of world confusion and degradation is nearing an end and a new Golden Age of the spirit will then begin.

NOTES ON THE
PSYCHIC REALITY

In the Hindu scheme of life spiritual time is divided
into 5000 year epochs, each composed of 4 cycles of 1250
years. Originally each cycle was made up of a different number
of years but time became averaged to make calculations easier.
Each cycle marks a change in the relationship between man
and his universe, the way the human psyche undergoes
changes in its spiritual journey toward nirvana. Each cycle
represents a progressive decline in piety and morality, then a
rebirth. The first 1250 years is the Golden Age. Man is in
harmony with his world of nature, a time when man functions
in a synergistic relationship with his physical environment that
is, appropriately, what ecology is all about. In the second
period, the Silver Age, mankind and his ego emerges and his
purity becomes tarnished. By the third period, the Copper
Age, man's spirit is adulterated and his occupations with self
obscure the true values of life and spirit. From this state he

enters the fourth period of the cycle, the Iron Age, a period of upward spiritual movement from its nadir, a period favorable to the renovations of the spirit, a time of resurrection of consciousness and a preparation for spiritual regeneration and rebirth into a new Golden Age that begins the 5000 year cycle all over again. (The idea of the cosmos passing through four similar cycles for all eternity was similarly developed in both ancient Greece and Persia.)

Now the spiritual grapevine is bursting with another rumor. It is said the universal clock is now at the end of the Iron Age and with its ending will come the next Golden Age when conditions are propitious for the fulfillment of man's karma. The last psychic epoch began and is now ending in India. The sages agree the Vedic understanding of the harmony between man and his universe is evolving in the United States. Most swamis want their teachings (and their souls?) to be already established in the United States when the next Golden Age arrives.

Centuries ago the time of the psychic evolutionary cycles stretched almost to infinity itself. In the hazy, magical history of India, long before she was persuaded to annotate time with dates and places, each period of the cycle was 4,320,000,000 earthly years—a single cosmic day of the god, when he creates the universe then absorbs it into his body to sleep through a cosmic night of equal length, when the universe is the potentiality to be created again on the next cosmic day. The entire cycle then lasted for 311,040,000,000 years (360 cosmic days and 360 cosmic nights).

It is part of the charm of India, part of the uncertainty of its reality, that its theories of the nature of the universe can be shaped to the problem at hand. Several quite discordant

theories can exist side by side in its cosmological structure. In
the case of the psychic cycles, the nuisance of dating historical
events revealed considerable discrepancy with the times indicated in the epics that told India's history. Changing god-
years to human-years matched up history and myth much more
satisfactorily.

As a matter of fact, the historians and the sages of
philosophy have calculated the god years to be of 1200 earthly
years, not 1250 years. Yet the cycle of 1250 years is most
commonly cited. This accomodation would likely be viewed
by the Westerner as a gross inaccuracy, despite its mythologi-
cal origin, yet such hard and fast rules of time and space are
of little consequence to a society evolved for the sole purpose
of the realization of the psychic self. This adjustment of earthly
fact with the psychic reality is a phenomenon peculiar to India,
a phenomenon that influences every facet of Indian life that is
still neither recognized nor acknowledged. The Indian, of
course, is not concerned by the adjustment since he lives in a
psychic world in which it is the *physical* world that is illusory.
It is the Westerner who cannot understand, to whom the
accomodation of physical nature to an unsubstantial psychic
arena is so impossible that it is not to be believed. And so
neither side acknowledges this fundamental difference in perspective. Moreover, the Indian sees no paradox in coping with
the physical world on *its* basis while at the same time being
confident that it doesn't exist.

It is in this accomodation of earthly to psychic reality
that history becomes bent toward mythology and myths are
adjusted to history and the scriptures of the sages. Hinduism
itself is an accomodation of an extraordinary number of

different views and approaches to the spiritual meaning of life, many so antithetical that the orderly logic of the Westerner collapses in despair. Indian history is almost equally a problem in sorting fact from fantasy and not a few historians question Indian beliefs about its early history.

Accordingly, there is a serious problem in the study of India's moods and life styles and about what is authoritative and what is not. The West prizes the precise documents and opinions of its authorities. But in India, there is little documentation and there are as many authorities as there are beliefs and differences in beliefs. What is important in understanding the Indian scene is not only understanding the reasons for incompatibilities in their belief systems (and hence the effect on their behavior), but also in understanding that by and large the dominant influence on Indian thought is its oral tradition.

There are a thousand reasons why oral history, oral story telling, and oral teachings of philosophy and religion are the forces that still shape and control Indian thought. India is perhaps 85% illiterate; the caste system still sequesters authority and the authorities are primarily concerned with the life of the spirit. Indian thought processes are traditionally mythic, not systematic, and prevailing thought affirms that it is not necessary for knowledge to come from outside the self for spiritual fulfillment. Although direct experience is held to be the only true path to enlightenment, the difficulty of the self-experience is also recognized and is the reason for the tradition of the guru (the guide).

And so it is that even in the 20th century, much of Indian belief, even among the most learned minds, rests upon word of mouth communication with all its inherent difficulties of exaggeration, fantasy, and errors of transmission. When this kind of communication exists alongside an extraordinary capacity for reconciling fact with fancy, there is little else to do but give folklore and rumor some validity, for it is the fact-and-fantasy blend that affects lives and determines behavior, not obscure written words.

This does not mean that India does not have as great a store of written philosophy as any other part of the world. There are thousands and thousands of still untranslated Sanscrit manuscripts left from India's beginnings. It is, rather, that scholars are limited in supply and fewer still have an inclination or feel a need to examine more philosophic texts than needed for their own devotions. The Tibetan lama and the Hindu holy man read the sages and meditate, meditate and reread the scriptures. The Hindu and the Buddhist believe that enlightenment comes from within, from the experience of contemplation and the struggle for enlightenment. It is the *scholars of the experiential* who teach, who become the gurus who dispense the wisdom of the Vedas. It is *not* the literati nor the experts in history or religion or the origins of religion who teach. Sri Ramakrishna, the founder of Vedanta in the late 1880s, for example, was virtually illiterate. His wisdom was said to come from God, and certainly to read it, much of it does seem god-knowing. There are millions of Vendantists around the globe today, many who are among the wisest and most profoundly knowledgeable in the world, who honor Ramakrishna's teachings. It was as if someone (Ramakrishna) had to fill in the gaps in philosophic theory, and those who did, did so by the spiritual experience. Do not, however, ever underestimate the intellectual prowess of the Indian. Indian science had developed a systematic medicine *and* surgery by 100 A.D. that rivals the Western medicine and surgery of today.

The Indian is concerned primarily with spiritual life and with the sole objective of achieving oneness with the cosmic consciousness. This concept of the spiritual life is also embraced, informally but wholly, by the majority of non-Hindus in India. It is said that long before writing evolved, the wise men who came out of the West to settle India had understood that the liberation of man could be obtained only by an evolving consciousness. With that principle in mind, just a look at the persistence of this fundamental principle of life along with awareness of the mind power of the massive population of India and it becomes clear that the belief man exists only to reach the consciousness of the universal underlies every thought and movement in India.

India was dealing with masses of people long before population became a problem in other lands. As noted earlier, Alexander of Greece estimated the subcontinent to have 100 million people by 4 A.D. Perhaps because of the population problem, the Indian theory of soul developed very early in its history, a theory fundamentally different from those that arose just to the West in Palestine and Egypt. The Hindu doctrine did not render the soul to God since the soul was already part of God. The Hindu doctrine deals directly with the primary question of man since his beginning: why life, why death?

It may have been because of the intimate harmony between primitive peoples and their environment that the concept of *samsara* arose, the concept that the soul repeatedly passes from life to life through eternity. This belief served to confirm not only man's relationship to his environment but also a feeling of identity with all of nature. Identity with nature was not enough, however, because the blessings and torments of nature were not always equally distributed. The practical solution to this problem was the evolution of the belief that one's lot in life was but one of many appearances of a soul on earth, and if the lot were miserable, there could always be a chance to improve it. The determining factor was the assiduousness with which one pursued the spiritual life. This belief became the principle of *karma,* literally meaning "deed", that one's actions in one life determined one's status in the next.

The idea that man could exert control over his spiritual destiny, that if his lot were miserable in one life, attention to spiritual progress could ensure a much happier lot in the next, eased the pain of the less fortunate and gave encouragement for continued spiritual development to the more fortunate. Although the caste system has become less and less appropriate, it was the adoption of caste divisions that made severe social injustices of one's hereditary fate tolerable.

Karma also extends to the profoundly comforting concept that one can ultimately escape the cycle of death and rebirth by fulfilling one's karma with devotional action and the striving to enter into Eternal Bliss.

No one is exempt from the karmic cycle. Unlike Western notions about the divine, the gods themselves can also die and be reborn, and their reincarnations to this day serve as living examples of both following the Path to union with the cosmic consciousness and manifestations of the state of consciousness that envelops man when he becomes enlightened.

Karma has come to have many different meanings. In the West it is popularly thought to mean destiny. But it is just not any destiny, it is the becoming one with cosmic consciousness more specifically, karma, "deeds", is the Path of action to the enlightenment that is knowing God, the Path of worshipful action. In the confusing labels of Hindu philosophy, the personal liberation of union with God is liberation from the bondage of karma, from the need to search and to act and do devotional deeds for the realization of the spiritual nature of man, to attain the enlightenment. To be released from one's karma is to have fulfilled one's karma. And for most human beings this can be achieved by acts of devotion, acts man must continue until he achieves realization, for he has no alternative.

It is strange that this book ends with reminders about karma (actually, the book seemed to end itself), but there seemed no better place to include a note about one of the deepest influences in Indian life. Immersed in contemplation about karma, I remembered my long preoccupation with my need to write about India. Throughout my long association with the land and peoples of India, I have felt an unremitting compulsion to do my bit to set the record straight about the essential nature of India. Too many voices around the world, including those in India, decry the apparent ignorance and poverty and inertia of its population. Still, from time to time, intellects of the world, from Jung to Huxley, have discovered spiritual and mental riches in the psychic nets of India. There was, I became convinced, evidence for these psychic nets, and ways to make them known. Finally I realized that my experiences across the broad reaches of India revealed something of the warp and woof of these nets and if I told my tales correctly, perhaps others might be touched by the psychic plenty that can be found by the open mind travelling in India.

INDEX